Risk Management

Principles and Techniques

Risk Management

Principles and Techniques

By

Uma Narang

Associate Professor,
Department of Commerce,
Post-graduate Government College, Chandigarh

New Century Publications
New Delhi, India

NEW CENTURY PUBLICATIONS
4800/24, Bharat Ram Road,
Ansari Road, Daryaganj,
New Delhi - 110 002 (India)

Tel.: 011-2324 7798, 4358 7398, 6539 6605
Fax: 011-4101 7798
E-mail: indiatax@vsnl.com • info@newcenturypublications.com
www.newcenturypublications.com

Editorial office:
LG–7, Aakarshan Bhawan,
4754-57/23, Ansari Road, Daryaganj,
New Delhi – 110 002

Tel.: 011-4356 0919

First Published: **July 2015**

ISBN: **978-81-7708-416-0**

Published by New Century Publications and printed at Salasar Imaging Systems, New Delhi.

Designs: Patch Creative Unit, New Delhi.

PRINTED IN INDIA

About the Book

Risk management refers to the practice of identifying potential risks in advance, analysing them and taking precautionary steps to mitigate/eliminate them. Thus, risk management is simply the practice of systematically identifying and understanding risks and the controls that are in place to manage them.

Risk is defined as the chance of something happening that will have an impact on objectives. Whatever may be the type of risk, there is a need to manage it. For this, there should be a risk management strategy which maximizes shareholders' risk-adjusted return. The management of risk is an integral part of good corporate governance. The primary reason for managing risk is to enable agencies to successfully achieve their goals.

Risk management ensures that an organization identifies and understands the risks to which it is exposed. Risk management also guarantees that an organization creates and implements an effective plan to prevent losses or reduce the impact, if a loss occurs. Risk management has assumed greater importance in the backdrop of failure of many banks globally.

This book explains and examines various aspects of risk management practices and strategies in areas concerning banking, foreign exchange, insurance and credit derivatives.

About the Author

Dr. Uma Narang is Associate Professor, Department of Commerce, Post-graduate Government College, Chandigarh. She did her M.Com. and Ph.D. from Panjab University, Chandigarh. With teaching experience of 17 years, she has published more than 15 papers in reputed national and international journals. She also has 2 books to her credit in the areas of accounting and micro credit institutions. She has participated and presented more than 22 papers at various national and international conferences/seminars. Her areas of academic interest include accounting, insurance and human resources management.

Contents

Preface

Risk is defined as 'the chance of something happening that will have an impact on objectives'. Whatever may be the type of risk, there is a need to manage it. For this, there should be risk management strategy which ultimately maximizes the shareholders' value and risk adjusted return, and to minimize volatility related to uncertainty. The management of risk is an integral part of good management practice.

Risk management can be applied to all levels of an organisation, in both the strategic and operational contexts, to specific projects, decisions and recognised risk areas. The primary reason for managing risk is to enable agencies to successfully achieve their goals.

Risk management refers to the practice of identifying potential risks in advance, analysing them and taking precautionary steps to mitigate/eliminate them. Thus, risk management is simply the practice of systematically identifying and understanding risks and the controls that are in place to manage them.

Risk management ensures that an organization identifies and understands the risks to which it is exposed. Risk management also guarantees that an organization creates and implements an effective plan to prevent losses or reduce the impact, if a loss occurs. Risk management also addresses many risks that are not insurable, including brand integrity, potential loss of tax-exempt status for volunteer groups, public goodwill etc.

Risk management has assumed greater importance in the backdrop of failure of many banks globally. Risk management is primarily concerned with reducing earnings volatility and avoiding large losses. Basel Committee on Banking Supervision (BCBS), consisting of experts in the field of banking and risk management, issued various guidelines under Basel-I, II and III, detailing the methodology for risk identification, assessment, monitoring, mitigating, controlling and reporting of various risks in the banks.

Risk management is critical for banking business. Although risk and return are directly proportional, it is imperative that risks should be held under control and return should be increased for achieving higher profitability in banks. As such, effective risk management insight by the top management, approved risk policies, procedure documents, risk management tools and internal control measures have become essential elements in the framework. Risk professionals are required to rejig their skills and knowledge continuously and constantly, so as to remain in total preparedness for facing any challenges posed by the risks. Risk is like fire, and the way we handle it, results in a positive or a negative impact on the business.

A major issue in establishing an appropriate risk management organisation structure is choosing between a centralised and decentralised structure. The primary responsibility of understanding the risks run by the bank and ensuring that the risks are appropriately managed should clearly be vested with the board of directors. A risk management organisation consists of:

- Board of directors.
- Risk management committee.
- Committee of senior level executives.
- Risk management support group.

In the process of risk management, the following elements should be taken into account:

- Risk identification.
- Risk measurement/quantification.
- Risk pricing.
- Risk control.
- Monitoring and reviewing.

Risk management can be considered as a very powerful strategic tool and has become more prevalent in recent decades due to rapid growth in industrial sector.

Traditionally, risk management was limited in scope to pure loss exposure, including liability risks, property risks etc. Further, its scope was expanded to include speculative financial risks.

Risk management tools include the following:

- Risk management information systems (RMIS).
- Value at risk (VaR) analysis.
- Risk maps.
- Catastrophic modelling.
- Websites.

RMIS is an information system that assists in consolidating property values, claims, policy, and exposure information and provides the tracking and management reporting capabilities to enable the user to monitor and control the overall cost of risk. RMIS is a computerized database that permits the risk manager to store and analyse risk management data and to use such data to predict and control future loss levels.

VaR is a popular technique in financial risk management analysis. VaR is the worst probable loss likely to occur in a given time period under regular market conditions at some level of confidence. VaR has been called the "new science of risk management". The concept is applied to a portfolio of assets, such as a mutual fund or a pension fund and is similar to the concept of 'maximum probable loss' in traditional property and liability risk management.

A risk map is a data visualization tool for communicating specific risks an organization faces. Risk maps deliver quality data that increases public awareness and leads to action that reduces risk to life and property. Risk maps are grids detailing the potential frequency and severity of risks faced by the organisation. The goal of a risk map is to improve an organization's understanding of its risk profile and appetite, clarify thinking on the nature and impact of risks, and improve the organization's risk assessment model.

Catastrophic modelling is the process of using computer-assisted calculations to estimate the losses that could be sustained due to a catastrophic event such as a hurricane or an earthquake. Input variables include such factors as meteorological data, historical losses and values exposed to loss (e.g., structures, population, etc.). The output from the computer analysis is an estimate of likely results from the occurrence of a catastrophic events such as cyclones, hurricanes, floods, earthquakes, terrorist attacks etc.

Risk management departments have developed their own websites, which include answers to frequently asked questions, and other related information. Earlier there were traditional risk management websites which have now been expanded in the form of a risk management intranet. An intranet is a website with search capabilities designed for a limited internal audience. An intranet is a computer network that uses internet protocol technology to share information, operational systems, or computing services within an organization. Intranets can serve as powerful tools for communication within an organization.

Chandigarh
June 2015

Uma Narang

1

Risk Management: Conceptual Framework

1.1 History of Risk Management

The roots of the risk management philosophy lie in the risk management failures of the past. These events range from the 17th century reasoning of a monk called Blaise Pascal to the Barings derivative scandal in 1995 with numerous events in between and running up to the present. The risks encountered were varied, challenging and complex, encompassing frauds, market crashes, political problems, and rogue traders to name a few.

During the 17th Century, Blaise Pascal suggested that it was less risky to believe in God than to be a non-believer. His line of reasoning went like this:

"If we believe in God and it turns out that there is no God, we will be not be worse for having believed. However, if we do not believe in God and there is a God, we may be punished for eternity for our stubbornness. In other words, it is less risky to believe in God…just in case"! This was also in some form a crude application of the laws of probability for predicting the likelihood of unwanted consequences.

Admittedly, risk management formally derived its origin from the insurance industry, as the earlier "risk managers" employed by mega corporations were charged merely with the responsibilities of maintaining a portfolio of insurance policies. This business of insurance-buying gradually became a significant and specialized function. The establishment of the Insurance Division by the American Management Association in 1931, the Insurance Buyers of New York (which later became the Risk Research Institute) in 1932, and the National Insurance Buyers Association are cases in point.

In the 1970s and 1980s, risk management as a thinking started to gain momentum. Importantly, contrary to its early focus on protecting against catastrophe and unaffordable potential losses, there was a distinct severance of risk management from the insurance discipline. The change of name of the National Insurance Buyers Association to the Risk and Insurance Management Society (RIMS) in 1975 clearly signalled this transition.

1.2 Why Risks Need to be Managed?

As we know that under the impact of uncertainties, variations in net cash flow take place which could be favourable as well as unfavourable. The possible unfavourable impact is the 'risk'. The loss potential of a business is strongly correlated to the uncertainties of the business factors as it is the outcome of their adverse impact. Therefore, the loss potential of a business is correlated to the risks in the business, and therefore, risk exposure of a business, needs to be managed so as to limit potential losses in adverse situations to a level that can be absorbed by organisations or banks without affecting their continuity. This aspect of risk management creates an imperative to develop methods to measure risk so that an organisation is aware of the risk it is carrying for its business, i.e. it has a measure of its potential losses in severely adverse situations and may ensure adequate capital availability for its continuance or limit its risk exposure to the extent of capital available.

It seems appropriate to begin with why these firms manage risks—for any discussion of risk management procedures. According to standard economic theory, managers of value maximizing firms ought to maximize expected profit without regard to the variability around its expected value. However, there is now a growing literature on the reasons for active risk management including the work of Stulz (1984), Smith, Smithson and Wolford (1990), and Froot, Sharfstein and Stein (1993), to name but a few of the more notable contributions.

In fact, the review of risk management reported in Santomero (1995) lists dozens of contributions to the area and at least four distinct rationales offered for active risk management. These include managerial self-interest, the non-linearity of the tax structure, the costs of financial distress and the existence of capital market imperfections. Any one of these justifies the firms' concern over return variability, as the aforementioned cited authors demonstrate. Thus, risk management requires special skills and knowledge that has an objective which is more oriented towards control aspect of the business—it not only requires a separate setup in the organisation but also needs a well-defined framework that guides the risk management function.

1.3 Risk Management Defined

Risk is defined as 'the chance of something happening that will have an impact on objectives'. It is, therefore, important to understand what the objectives of an organisation, faculty, work unit or position of an individual are, prior to attempting to analyse the risks. In actual practice, whatever may be the type of risk, there is a need to manage the risks. For this, there should be risk management strategy which ultimately maximizes the shareholders' value and risk adjusted return, and minimizes volatility related to uncertainty. The management of risk is an integral part of good management practice.

Risk management is defined in standard as 'the systematic application of management policies, procedures and practices to the tasks of establishing the context, identifying, analyzing, assessing, treating, monitoring and communicating'. It is an iterative process that, with each cycle, can contribute progressively to organisational improvement by providing management with a greater insight into risks and their impact.

Risk management can be applied to all levels of an organisation, in both the strategic and operational contexts, to specific projects, decisions and recognised risk areas. The primary reason for managing risk is to enable agencies to successfully achieve their goals. Risk management refers to the practice of identifying potential risks in advance, analysing them and taking precautionary steps to reduce/curb the risk. To put it otherwise, it is the process of identification, analysis and either acceptance or mitigation of uncertainty in investment decision-making. Essentially, risk management occurs anytime an investor or fund manager analyses and attempts to quantify the potential for losses in an investment and then takes the appropriate action (or inaction) given their investment objectives and risk tolerance. Inadequate risk management can result in severe consequences for companies as well as individuals. Thus, risk management is simply the practice of systematically identifying and understanding risks and the controls that are in place to manage them.

Risk management ensures that an organization identifies and understands the risks to which it is exposed. Risk management also guarantees that the organization creates and implements an effective plan to prevent losses or reduce the impact if a loss occurs. Risk management also addresses many risks that are not insurable, including brand integrity, potential loss of tax-exempt status for volunteer groups, public goodwill etc.

Risk management is the identification, analysis, assessment, control, avoidance, minimization, and elimination of unacceptable risks. An organisation may use risk assumption, risk avoidance, risk retention, risk transfer, or any other strategy (or combination of strategies) in proper fashion for future events.

'Risk management is defined as the logical development and carrying out of a plan to deal with potential losses. The purpose of a risk management programme is to manage an organisation's exposure to loss and to protect its assets' (Mark S. Dorsman).

Risk management evaluates which risks, identified in the risk assessment process, require management and selects and implements the plans or actions that are required to ensure that those risks are controlled.

According to Wason (2005), general strategies for managing risks include:

- Avoid—eliminate, stop, prohibit or sell the risk exposure.
- Retain—accept and self-insure the risk exposure (i.e. by integrating it with other risks or by diversifying risks).
- Reduce—mitigate or cap portions of risk exposure.
- Transfer—hedging or outsourcing of risk exposure.

Risk management is a process that identifies loss exposures faced by an organisation and selects the most appropriate techniques for treating such exposures. As an integrated process, it involves few logical steps such as: (a) defining the objectives of the risk management exercise; (b) identifying the risk exposures; (c) evaluating the exposures; (d) critical analysis of risk management alternatives and selecting one of them; and (e) implementation and review. Conditions under which firms operate change—the risk management process, therefore has a necessity to be dynamic.

1.4 Risk Management Framework

Risk management has assumed greater importance in the backdrop of failure of many banks globally. Risk management is primarily concerned with reducing earnings volatility and avoiding large losses. Basel Committee on Banking Supervision (BCBS) consisting of experts in the field of banking and risk management issued various guidelines under Basel-I, II and III, detailing the methodology for risk identification, assessment, monitoring, mitigating, controlling and reporting of various risks in the banks. Besides, it also entails imposing supervisory responsibility on the local regulator [like Reserve Bank of India (RBI) in India], to ensure the implementation of risk management framework in banks. In the background of these developments, RBI issued comprehensive guidelines relating to risk management framework to be introduced in the banks in a time bound schedule.

Risk management is critical for banking business.

Although risk and return are directly proportional, it is imperative that risks should held under control and return should be increased for achieving higher profitability in banks. As such, effective risk management oversight by the top management, approved risk policies, procedure documents, risk management tools and internal control measures have become essential elements in the framework. Risk professionals are required to rejig their skill and knowledge continuously and constantly, so as to remain in total preparedness for facing any challenges posed by the risks. Risk is like fire, and the way we handle it, results in a positive or a negative impact on banking business. Following are the basic considerations that should be taken into account for designing a risk management framework in an organisation:

1. Management of risk is a major concern of top management. Successful implementation of risk management process emanates from the top management and the main challenge centres on facilitating implementation of risk and business policies simultaneously in a consistent manner. Modern best practices consist of setting risk limits, based on economic measures of risk while ensuring best risk adjusted return, keeping in view the capital that has been invested in the business.
2. Risk management begins with identification and its quantification. It is only after risks are identified and measured that we may decide to accept the risk or to accept the risk at a reduced level by undertaking steps to mitigate the risk, either fully or partially.
3. Risk management happens to be a job that requires special skills and has an objective which is more oriented towards control aspect of the business—it requires a separate setup in an organisation.

According to the RBI circular issued on risk management, the broad parameters of risk management function should encompass:

1. Organisational structure.

2. Comprehensive risk measurement approach.
3. Risk management policies approved by the Board which should be consistent with the broader business strategies, capital strength, management expertise and overall willingness to assume risk.
4. Guidelines and other parameters used to govern risk taking, including detailed structure of prudential limits.
5. Strong MIS for reporting, monitoring and controlling risks.
6. Well laid out procedures, effective control and comprehensive risk reporting framework.
7. Separate risk management framework, independent of operational departments and with clear delineation of levels of responsibility for management of risk.
8. Periodical review and evaluation.

Risk management framework covers areas such as: (i) organisation for risk management; (ii) risk identification; (iii) risk measurement; (iv) risk pricing; (v) risk monitoring and control; and (v) risk mitigation.

1.5 Risk Management Organisation

A major issue in establishing an appropriate risk management organisation structure is choosing between a centralised and decentralised structure. The primary responsibility of understanding the risks run by the bank and ensuring that the risks are appropriately managed should clearly be vested with the board of directors. The risk management organisation consists of:

- The board of directors.
- The risk management committee.
- The committee of senior level executives.
- Risk management support group.

The board of directors have the overall responsibility for the management of risks. The board articulates risk management policies, procedures, aggregate risk limits, review mechanism and reporting and auditing systems. The board should decide the risk management policy of the bank and set limits for various risks.

Risk management committee is a board level sub-committee. The responsibilities of risk management committee with regard to risk management aspects include the following:

- Setting guidelines for risk management and reporting.
- Ensuring that risk management processes conforms to the policy.
- Setting up prudential limits and their periodical reviews.
- Ensuring robustness of risk management models.
- Ensuring proper manning for the processes.

The committee of senior level executives is responsible for implementation of risk and business policies simultaneously, in a consistent manner and decides on the business strategy to achieve these objectives. It also sets up operating limits and is the review authority for the line management. The purpose of this top level committee is to empower one group with full responsibility of evaluating overall risks faced by a bank and determining the level of risks which will be in the best interest of the bank. Risk management support group analysis monitors and reports the risk profiles to the committee of senior level executives. It also examines the effects of various possible changes in market variables and recommends the action needed. They are also responsible for the critical functions of independent risk monitoring, measurement, analysis and reporting.

In addition to the aforementioned measures, there is a need to enrich the organisational risk culture by sharing risk management knowledge and skills through training and development initiatives which will reap long-term benefits for the bank.

1.6 Process of Risk Management

To overcome the risk and to make banking function well, there is a need to manage all kinds of risks associated with the banking. Risk management becomes one of the main functions of any banking services. Risk management consists of identifying the risk and controlling them—meaning, keeping the risks at acceptable level. These levels differ from institution to institution and country to country. The basic objective of risk management is to enhance the stakeholders' value by maximising the profit and optimizing the capital funds for ensuring long-term solvency of the banking organisation. The process of risk management comprises of the following functions:

- Risk identification.
- Risk measurement/quantification.
- Risk pricing.
- Risk control.
- Monitoring and reviewing.

1.6.1 Risk Identification: All transactions undertaken would have one or more of the major risks, i.e., liquidity risk, interest rate risk, credit risk, market risk and operational risk. The impact of risk taking at transaction level on the portfolio risk is a critical issue. Because certain risks such as liquidity risk and interest rate risk are managed at the aggregate or portfolio level, risks such as credit risk, operational risk and market risk arising from individual transactions are taken cognizance of at the transaction as well as at the portfolio level. In essence, risk identification consists of identifying various risks associated with risk taking at the transaction level and examining its impact on the portfolio level and on the capital requirement. Risk identification involves:

- Understanding the nature of various kinds of risks.
- Circumstances which lead to a situation to become a risk situation.
- Causes due to which the risk can arise.

1.6.2 Risk Measurement or Quantification: Risk quantification is an assessment of the degree of the risk which a particular transaction or an activity is exposed to. Though the exact measurement of risk is not possible but the level of risk can be determined with the help of risk rating models. Risk management relies on quantitative measures of risk. The risk measures seek to capture variations in earnings, market value, losses due to default etc. (referred to as target variables), arising out of uncertainties associated with various risk elements. Quantitative measures of risks can be classified into three categories: (a) based on sensitivity, (b) based on volatility, and (c) based on downside potential.

Sensitivity captures deviation of a target due to unit movement of a single market parameter. Only those market parameters, which drive the value of the target variable, are relevant for the purpose. Usually, market risk models use sensitivities fairly widely.

Volatility is the standard deviation of the values of the variable such as earnings. Standard deviation is the square root of the variance of the random variable.

It is feasible to calculate historical volatility using any set of historical data, whether or not they follow a normal distribution. Volatility helps us to capture possible variations around the average of the target variables, both upside and downside.

Downside potential is the most comprehensive measure of risk as it integrates sensitivity and volatility with the adverse effect of uncertainty. It has two components—potential losses and probability of occurrence. This is the measure that is most relied upon by banking and financial services industry, as also the regulators.

1.6.3 Risk Pricing: In banking transactions, risks have two-fold impacts. Firstly, banks have to maintain necessary capital, at least as per regulatory requirements. The capital required is not without costs. The cost of capital arises from the need to pay investors in bank's equity and for internal generation of capital necessary for business growth. Each banking transaction should be able to generate necessary surplus to meet this cost. The pricing of transaction must take that into account. Secondly, there is a probability of loss associated with all risks. This also needs to be factored into pricing.

Risk pricing implies factoring risks into pricing through

charge and loss probabilities. This would be in addition to the actual costs incurred in the transaction. The actual costs incurred are the cost of funds that has gone into the transaction and costs incurred in giving the services, which are incurred by way of maintaining the infrastructure, employees and other relevant expenses. Pricing, therefore, should take into account the following:

- Cost of deployable funds.
- Operating expenses.
- Loss probabilities.
- Capital charge.

It should be kept in mind that the cost of funds should correspond to the term for which it is deployed. This is because five year funds may have a different cost than a one year fund due to time value of money.

1.6.4 Risk Control: Risk control is the stage where the banks or institutions take steps to control the risk with the help of various tools. Since risks arise from uncertainties associated with the risk elements, risk reduction is achieved by adopting strategies that eliminate or reduce the uncertainties associated with the risk elements. This is known as risk mitigation. Risk mitigation measures aim to reduce downside variability in net cash flow but they also reduce upside potential simultaneously. There is a need to deploy various techniques to mitigate the risks. There is a need to depute certain competent officers in order to deal with such risks. Following are the few techniques for risk control:

- Diversification of the business.
- Insurance and hedging.
- Fixation of exposure ceiling.
- Transfer the risk to another party at the right time.
- Securitisation and reconstruction.

1.6.5 Risk Monitoring: In risk monitoring, the bankers have to fix up the parameters on which the transaction is to be tested, to be sure that there is no risk to viable existence of the financial unit or investment of the bank. Modern best practices consist of setting risk limits based on economic measures of risk while ensuring best risk adjusted return, keeping in view the risks and returns and that too within the constraints of available capital. In order to achieve these objectives, banks must put in place the following:

- An organisational structure.
- Comprehensive risk measurement approach.
- Risk management policies adopted at the corporate level, which are consistent with the broader business strategies, capital strength, management expertise and risk appetite.
- Guidelines and other parameters used to govern risk taking, including detailed structure of prudential limits, discretionary limits and risk taking functions.

The feedback of the actual functioning is therefore necessary for the purpose of control. Thus, banks should establish an adequate system for monitoring and reporting risk exposures and assessing bank's changing risk profile. The bank's senior management or board of directors should on a regular basis, receive reports on the bank's risk profile and capital needs. The banks should conduct periodic reviews of its risk management process to ensure its integrity, accuracy and reasonableness.

1.7 Rules of Risk Management

1. There is a need to assess the risk/return ratio.
2. Continuously identify and assess the risks.
3. Risk is measured and managed by people, not mathematical models.
4. In risk, there is a need to know what you do not know.
5. Risks should be discussed openly.
6. Risk must be diversified because multiple risks will produce more consistent rewards.
7. There is a need to show discipline because a consistent and rigorous approach will beat a constantly changing strategy.
8. Use common sense as it is better to be approximately right than being precisely wrong.

9. Return is only half the equation because risk as well as the return needs to be considered when making decisions.

1.8 Objectives of Risk Management

Risk management can be considered as a very powerful strategic tool and has become more prevalent in recent decades due to rapid growth in industrial sector. Risks can be uncertainty in financial markets, failure of projects, legal liabilities, credit risk, accidents of natural causes and disasters, etc. Risk management facilitates an organisation to avoid huge financial losses, resulting into bankruptcy. It helps in protecting employees from accidents that might result in death or injury. Risk management has important objectives such as pre-loss objectives and post-loss objectives. Pre-loss objectives include: (i) to prepare for potential loss; (ii) to reduce anxiety; and (iii) to meet any legal obligations. Post-loss objectives include: (i) survival of the firm; (ii) to continue operating; (iii) stability of earnings; (iv) to minimize the effects that a loss will have on other persons and on the society; and (v) continued growth of the firm. The other objectives are:

- To identify and prioritize potential risk events.
- Help develop risk management strategies and risk management plans.
- Use established risk management methods, tools and techniques to assist in the analysis and reporting of identified risk events.
- Find ways to identify and evaluate risks.
- Develop strategies and plans for lasting risk management strategies.

Traditionally, risk management was limited in scope to pure loss exposure, including liability risks, property risks etc. Its scope was further expanded to include speculative financial risks also.

1.9 Risk Management Tools

- Risk management information systems (RMIS).

- Value at risk (VaR) analysis.
- Risk maps.
- Catastrophic modelling.
- Websites.

1.9.1 Risk Management Information System (RMIS): RMIS is an information system that assists in consolidating property values, claims, policy, and exposure information and provides the tracking and management reporting capabilities to enable the user to monitor and control the overall cost of risk. Risk management information system is a computerized database that permits the risk manager to store and analyse risk management data and to use such data to predict and attempt to control future loss levels. A detailed list is prepared for record purpose. The management of risk data and information is a key to success of any risk management effort, regardless of an organization's size or industry sector. Risk management information systems/services (RMIS) are used to support expert advice and cost-effective information management solutions around key processes such as:

- Risk identification and assessment.
- Risk control.
- Risk financing.

RMIS facilitates the consolidation of information related to insurance, such as claims from multiple sources, property values, policy information, and exposure information, into one system. Often, RMIS applies primarily to 'casualty' claims/loss data systems. Such casualty coverages include auto liability, auto physical damage, workers' compensation, general liability and products liability.

Most major insurance companies (carriers), broker/agents, and third party administrators (TPAs) offer/provide at least one external RMIS product to the insured (clients) and any brokers involved in the insurance programme.

RMIS products are designed to provide the insured organizations and their brokers with basic policy and claim information via electronic access, and most recently, via the internet. This information is essential for managing individual claims, identifying trends, marketing an insurance programme, loss forecasting, actuarial studies and internal loss data communication within a client organization. They may also provide the tracking and management reporting capabilities to enable one to monitor and control the overall cost of risk in an efficient and cost-effective manner.

1.9.2 Value at Risk (VaR) Analysis: Value at risk (VaR) is a popular technique in financial risk management analysis. VaR is the worst probable loss likely to occur in a given time period under regular market conditions at some level of confidence. Value at risk (VaR) has been called the 'new science of risk management'. The concept is applied to a portfolio of assets, such as a mutual fund or a pension fund and is similar to the concept of 'maximum probable loss' in traditional property and liability risk management. The most popular and traditional measure of risk is volatility. The main problem with volatility, however, is that it does not care about the direction of an investment's movement—a stock can be volatile because it suddenly jumps higher. Thus, value at risk is used for this because it is applicable to stocks, bonds, currencies, derivatives, or any other assets with price.

VaR is a number, measured in price units or as a percentage of portfolio value, which tells you that in a defined large percentage of cases (usually 95 percent or 99 percent) *your portfolio is likely to not lose more* than that amount of money. Or said the other way around, in a defined small percentage of cases (5 percent or 1 percent) *your loss is expected to be greater than* that number.

Largest loss likely to be suffered on a portfolio position over a holding period (usually 1 to 10 days) with a given probability (confidence level), VAR is a measure of market risk, and is equal to one standard deviation of the distribution of possible returns on a portfolio of positions.

VaR is just one number giving a *rough idea* about the *extent of risk in the portfolio*. VaR is measured in price units (dollars, euros) or as a percentage of portfolio value. This makes VaR very easy to interpret and to further use in analysis, which is one of the biggest advantages of VaR.

It is based on the probability distribution for a portfolio's market value. All liquid assets have uncertain market values, which can be characterized with probability distributions. All sources of market risk contribute to those probability distributions. Being applicable to all liquid assets and encompassing, at least in theory, all sources of market risk, value-at-risk is a broad metric of market risk. VaR provides quantitative and synthetic measures of risk, that allow to take into account, various kinds of cross-dependence between asset returns, fat-tail and non-normality effects, arising from the presence of financial options or default risk.

Value at risk can also be employed to examine the risk of insolvency for insurers. VaR can be determined in a number of ways, including using historical data and running a computer simulation.

1.9.3 Risk Maps: A risk map is a data visualization tool for communicating specific risks an organization faces. Risk maps deliver quality data that increases public awareness and leads to action that reduces risk to life and property.

Risk maps are grids detailing the potential frequency and severity of risks faced by the organisations. The goal of a risk map is to improve an organization's understanding of its risk profile and appetite, clarify thinking on the nature and impact of risks, and improve the organization's risk assessment model. Construction of these maps requires risk managers to analyse each risk that the organisation faces before plotting it on the map.

Use of maps varies from simply graphing the exposures to employing simulation analysis to estimate the likely loss scenarios. In addition to property, liability and personal exposures, financial risks and other risks that fall under the broad umbrella of enterprise risk may be included on the risk map. Thus, risk mapping is used to assist in identifying, prioritizing, and quantifying (at a macro level) risks to an organization.

1.9.4 Catastrophic Modelling: Catastrophic modelling is the process of using computer-assisted calculations to estimate the losses that could be sustained due to a catastrophic event such as a hurricane or earthquake. Input variables include such factors as meteorological data, historical losses and values exposed to loss (e.g., structures, population etc.). The output from the computer analysis is an estimate of likely results from the occurrence of a catastrophic event such as a category of 5 minute hurricane. Catastrophes such as cyclones, hurricanes, floods, earthquakes, terrorist attacks are rare events (from a statistical point of view) that cause losses and human suffering over large geographical areas. Insurance companies build models of these events both for underwriting, where they need estimates of local risk at various locations, and portfolio management, where it is imperative for them to estimate the correlation of risk at different locations and also have a means for aggregating the risk.

Cat modelling is especially applicable to analyzing risks in the insurance industry and is at the confluence of actuarial science, engineering, and meteorology. Catastrophe risk modelling provides essential data for global and regional insurers, reinsurers, brokers, financial markets and corporations to evaluate the potential and probability of risk and financial loss from natural hazards.

Insurers and risk managers use cat modelling to assess the risk in a portfolio of exposures. This might help guide an insurer's underwriting strategy or help them decide how much to reinsure to purchase. Some regulators allow insurers to use cat modelling in their rate filings to help determine how much premium their policyholders are charged in catastrophe-prone areas. Rating agencies such as A.M. Best and Standard and Poor's, use cat modelling to assess the financial strength of insurers that take on catastrophe risk. Reinsurers and reinsurance brokers also use cat modelling in the pricing and structuring of reinsurance treaties. Thus, these models are helpful tools and are employed by insurers, brokers, rating agencies and large companies with exposure to catastrophic losses.

1.9.5 Websites and Intranet: Risk management departments have developed their own websites, which include answers to 'frequently asked questions', and other related information. Earlier, there were traditional risk management websites which have now been expended in the form of a risk management intranet. An intranet is a website with search capabilities designed for a limited, internal audience. An intranet is a computer network that uses internet protocol technology to share information, operational systems, or computing services within an organization. With the help of intranet, employees can get a list of procedures to follow (formulated by the risk management department) along with a set of forms that must be signed and filed before the event can be held. Intranets can serve as powerful tools for communication within an organization—vertically strategic initiatives that have a global reach throughout the organization.

The type of information that can easily be conveyed is the purpose of the initiative and what the initiative is aiming to achieve, who is driving the initiative, results achieved till date, and who to speak to for more information. By providing this information on the intranet, the staff has the opportunity to keep up-to-date with the strategic focus of the organization. Some examples of communication would be chat, email, and/or blogs. A great real world example of where an intranet helped a company communicate is of Nestle which had a number of food processing plants in Scandinavia. Their central support system had to deal with a number of queries every day.

1.10 Risk Management and Derivatives

The last two decades have witnessed many-fold increase in the volume of international trade and business due to the ever-growing wave of globalization, openness and liberalization sweeping across the world. As a result, financial markets have experienced rapid variations in interest and exchange rates, stock market prices, thus exposing the corporate world to a state of growing financial risk. Increased financial risk causes losses to an otherwise profitable organisation. This underlines the importance of risk management to hedge against uncertainty.

Derivatives provide an effective solution to the problem of risk caused by uncertainty and volatility in an underlying asset. Derivatives are risk management tools that help an organisation to effectively transfer risk. Derivatives are instruments which have no independent value. Their value depends upon the underlying asset. The underlying asset may be financial or non-financial.

1.10.1 Emergence of Complex Financial Products: In recent years, complex financial products such as asset-backed securities, derivatives, credit-default swaps (CDSs) and collateralised debt obligations (CDOs) have proliferated in developed countries. These products have become highly popular with banks and financial institutions as they allow them to hedge their risks and manage their regulatory and economic capital more efficiently.

Although various structured products have enabled the transfer of risks and enhanced the liquidity of instruments, the 2008 turmoil in the US sub-prime mortgage market and related developments connected with complex derivatives have also brought to the fore the risks posed by these instruments.

The emergence of the market for derivative products, most notably forwards, futures and options, can be traced back to the willingness of risk-averse economic agents to guard themselves against uncertainties arising out of fluctuations in asset prices. By their very nature, the financial markets are marked by a very high degree of volatility. Through the use of derivative products, it is possible to partially or fully transfer price risks by locking-in asset prices. As instruments of risk management, derivatives generally do not influence the fluctuations in the underlying asset prices. However, by locking-in asset prices, derivative products minimize the impact of fluctuations in asset prices on the profitability and cash flow situation of risk-averse investors.

Derivative products initially emerged as hedging devices against fluctuations in commodity prices and commodity-linked derivatives remained the sole form of such products for a long time. The financial derivatives came into spotlight in post-1970 period due to growing instability in the financial markets. However, since their emergence, financial derivatives have become very popular and by 1990s, they accounted for about two-thirds of total transactions in derivative products. In recent years, the market for financial derivatives has grown tremendously both in terms of variety of instruments available, their complexity and also the turnover.

In India also, financial products such as mortgage-backed securities (MBS) and asset-backed securities (ABS) are in existence. Besides the securitised products, the Indian forex and rupee derivative markets have also developed significantly over the years.

In respect of forex derivatives involving Rupee, residents have access to foreign exchange forward contracts, foreign currency-Rupee swap instruments and currency options—both cross-currency and foreign currency-Rupee. As stated in the Annual Policy Statement for the year 2008-09, the Reserve Bank of India (RBI) announced the introduction of currency futures in the eligible exchanges for which the broad framework was announced in August 2008. In future, some more innovative and complex products might emerge. These products may pose several regulatory and supervisory challenges.

1.10.2 Derivatives Defined: Derivative in mathematics means a variable derived from another variable. The term *derivative* indicates that it has no independent value, i.e. its value is entirely *derived* from the value of the underlying asset. The underlying asset can be security, commodity, bullion, currency, livestock or anything else. In other words, derivative means a forward, future, option or any other hybrid contract of pre-determined fixed duration, linked for the purpose of contract fulfilment to the value of a specified real or financial asset of an index of securities. Similarly, in the financial sense, a derivative is a financial product, which has been derived from a market for another product. Without the underlying product, derivatives do not have any independent existence in the market.

Derivative instruments are defined by the Indian Securities Contracts (Regulation) Act, 1956 to include: (i) a security derived from a debt instrument, share, secured/unsecured loan, risk instrument or contract for differences, or any other form of security, and (ii) a contract that derives its value from the prices/index of prices of underlying securities.

In other words, derivatives are financial instruments whose value depends upon the value of an underlying asset. Since their value is essentially derived out of an underlying asset, they are financial abstractions whose value is derived mathematically from the changes in the value of the underlying asset.

The International Monetary Fund (IMF) defines derivatives as, "financial instruments that are linked to a specific financial instrument or indicator or commodity and through which specific financial risks can be traded in financial markets in their own right. The value of a financial derivative derives from the price of an underlying item, such as an asset or an index. Unlike debt securities, no principal is advanced to be repaid and no investment income accrues".

Derivatives have come into being because of the existence of risks in business. Thus, derivatives are means of managing risks. The parties managing risks in the market are known as *hedgers*. Some people/organizations are in the business of taking risks to earn profits. Such entities represent the *speculators*. The third player in the market known as the *arbitragers,* take advantage of the market mistakes.

In recent years, derivatives have become increasingly

important in the field of finance. While futures and options are now actively traded on many exchanges, forward contracts are popular on the over-the-counter (OTC) market.

1.10.3 Why are Derivatives Popular? Financial derivatives have become popular due to the following reasons:

1. Increased volatility in asset prices in financial markets.
2. Increased integration of national financial markets with the international markets.
3. Marked improvement in communication facilities and sharp decline in their costs.
4. Development of more sophisticated risk management tools, providing economic agents a wider choice of risk management strategies.
5. Innovations in the derivatives markets, which optimally combine the risks and returns over a large number of financial assets, leading to higher returns, reduced risk as well as transaction costs as compared to individual financial assets.

In the class of equity derivatives, futures and options on stock indices have gained more popularity than on individual stocks, especially among institutional investors, who are major users of index-linked derivatives. Even small investors find these useful due to high correlation of the popular indices with various portfolios and ease of use. The lower costs associated with index derivatives vis-à-vis derivative products based on individual securities is another reason for their growing use.

1.10.4 Types of Derivative Contracts: Derivative contracts have several variants. The most common variants are forwards, futures, options and swaps.

A. Forwards/Forward Contracts: A forward contract is a customised contract between two entities, where settlement takes place on a specific date in the future at today's pre-agreed price. A forward contract is an agreement to buy or sell an asset on a specified date for a specified price. One of the parties to the contract assumes a long position and agrees to buy the underlying asset on a certain specified future date, for a certain specified price. The other party assumes a short position and agrees to sell the asset on the same date for the same price. Other contract details like delivery date, price and quantity are negotiated bilaterally by the parties to the contract.

Forward contracts are normally traded outside stock exchanges. They are popular on the over the counter (OTC) market.

The salient features of forward contracts are as follows:

1. They are bilateral contracts and hence exposed to counter party risk.
2. Each contract is customer designed, and, hence, is unique in terms of contract size, expiration date and the asset type and quality.
3. The contract price is generally not available in public domain.
4. On the expiration date, the contract has to be settled by delivery for the asset.
5. If a party wishes to reverse the contract, it has to compulsorily go to the same counterparty, which often results in a high price being charged.

Forward contracts are very useful in hedging and speculation. A typical hedging application may pertain to an exporter who expects to receive payment in US dollars, 2 months later. He is exposed to the risk of exchange rate fluctuations. By using the currency forward market to sell Dollars forward, he can lock-on a rate today and reduce his uncertainty. Likewise, an importer who is required to make a payment in US dollars 2 months hence can reduce his exposure to exchange rate fluctuations by buying Dollars forward.

B. Futures/Future Contracts: Future contracts are special types of forward contracts in the sense that the former are standardised exchange-traded contracts. Future contract markets are designed to solve the problems that exist in forward markets. A future contract is an agreement between two parties to buy or sell an asset at a certain time in future, at a certain price. However, unlike forward contracts, future contracts are standardized and stock exchange-traded. To facilitate liquidity in the future contracts, the exchange specifies certain standard features for the contract. It is a standardized contract with a standard underlying instrument, a standard quantity and quality of the underlying instrument that can be delivered, and a standard timing of such settlement. A future contract may be offset prior to maturity by entering into an equal and opposite transaction. The standardized items in a future contract are the following:

1. Quantity of the underlying.
2. Quality of the underlying.
3. Date/month of delivery.
4. Units of price quotation and minimum price change.
5. Location of settlement.

C. Options: Options are fundamentally different from forward and future contracts. An option gives the holder of the option the right to do something. The holder does not have to necessarily exercise this right. In contrast, in a forward or future contract, the two parties commit themselves to doing something. Whereas it costs nothing (except margin requirements) to enter into a future contract, the purchase of an option requires an upfront payment.

Options are of two types: calls options and put options. Calls options give the buyer the right but not the obligation to buy a given quantity of the underlying asset, at a given price on or before a given future date. Put options give the buyer the right, but not the obligation to sell a given quantity of the underlying asset at a given price on or before a given date.

(a) Warrants: Options generally have lives of up to 1 year—the majority of options traded on options exchanges having maximum maturity of 9 months. Longer-dated options are called *warrants* and are generally traded over-the-counter.

(b) LEAPS: The acronym LEAPS means Long-term Equity Anticipation Securities. These are options having a maturity of up to 3 years.

(c) Baskets: Basket options are options on portfolios of underlying assets. The underlying asset is usually a moving average or a basket of assets. Equity index options are a form of basket options.

D. Swaps: Swaps are private agreements between two parties to exchange cash flows in the future according to a pre-arranged formula. They can be regarded as portfolios of forward contracts. Following are the two commonly used swaps:

(a) Interest Rate Swaps: These entail swapping of only the interest-related cash flows between the parties in the same currency.

(b) Currency Swaps: These entail swapping of both principal and interest between the parties, with the cash flows in one direction being in a different currency than those in the opposite direction.

E. Swaptions: Swaptions are options to buy or sell a swap that will become operative at the expiry of the options. Thus, swaption is an option on a forward swap. Rather than have call options and put options, the swaptions market has receiver swaptions and payer swaptions.

1.10.5 Participants in the Derivatives Market: The following three broad categories of participants, viz. hedgers, speculators, and arbitrageurs trade in the derivatives market.

A. Hedgers: Hedgers face risk associated with the price of an asset. They use future or option markets to reduce or eliminate this risk. In other words, hedgers are those who wish to protect their existing exposures and essentially are safety-driven.

B. Speculators: They bet on future movements in the price of an asset. Future and option contracts can give them an extra leverage; that is, they can increase both the potential gains and potential losses in a speculative venture. Speculators are willing risk takers who are expectation-driven.

C. Arbitrageurs: They are in business to take advantage of a discrepancy between prices in two different markets. If, for example, they see the futures price of an asset getting out of line with the cash price, they will take offsetting positions in the two markets to lock-in a profit. Arbitragers are traders and market-makers who deal in buying and selling derivatives contracts, hoping to profit from price-differentials between different markets. A market maker is one who provides two-way quotes for a given product and thereby runs a position in that product.

1.11 Changing Scenario of Risk Management

In insurance, the risk management is a tool, identifying business opportunities to design and modify the insurance products. In early days, risk management was limited to pure loss exposures, including property risks, personnel risk and liability risks. In early 1990s, an emerging trend emerged and various developments helped many businesses. As a result, the scope of risk management also expanded and all risks faced by the organisations have been considered under the risk management programmes. In addition to the utility for insurance underwriting business, risk management consultancy services are considered as value addition to the clients of insurance companies.

Risk assessment, the main part of the risk management process, is helpful in evaluation. The property, interruption and liability related risks are keenly looked at by the insurers. The risk management services like underwriting inspections or post-loss inspections for settlement claims are used by them in India. In addition to these, Loss Prevention Association of India and Tariff Advisory Committee provide full support to the insurance companies. The de-tariffication has further necessitated the use of risk services in insurance companies, broking houses as well as single entity firms. Some important risk assessment tools such as safety related audits, risk based audits, elementary risk audits etc. have been used.

Thus, risk management is a continuous process which runs throughout the organisation's strategy and the implementation of that strategy. It must be integrated with the culture of the organisation with proper and effective policy and full support from the top management.

2

Operational Risks

2.1 Background

Until Basel II reforms for banking supervision, operational risk was a residual category reserved for risks and uncertainties which were difficult to quantify and manage in traditional ways—the 'other risks' basket. Such regulations institutionalized operational risk as a category of regulatory and managerial attention and connected operational risk management with good corporate governance. Of course, businesses in general, and other institutions such as the military, have been aware, for many years, of hazards arising from operational factors, internal or external. The primary goal of the military is to fight and win wars in quick and decisive fashion, and with minimal losses. For the military, and the businesses of the world alike, operational risk management is an effective process for preserving resources by anticipation.

Following the two decades (from 1980s to the early 2000) of globalisation and deregulation, combined with the increased sophistication of financial services around the world, have introduced additional complexities into the activities of banks, insurers and firms in general and therefore their risk profiles. Since the mid-1990s, the topics of market risk and credit risk have been the subject of much debate and research, with the result that financial institutions have made significant progress in the identification, measurement and management of both these forms of risk.

However, the near collapse of the U.S. financial system in September 2008 is an indication that the ability to measure market and credit risk is far from perfect and eventually led to introduction of new regulatory requirements worldwide, including Basel III regulations for banks and Solvency II regulations for insurers. Similarly, the Committee is proposing to encompass explicitly risks other than credit and market in the New Basel Capital Accord. This proposal reflects the Committee's interest in making the New Basel Capital Accord more risk sensitive and the realisation that risks other than credit and market can be substantial. Further, developing banking practices such as securitisation, outsourcing, specialised processing operations and reliance on rapidly evolving technology and complex financial products and strategies suggest that these other risks are increasingly important factors to be reflected in credible capital assessments both by supervisors and the banks.

Under the 1988 Accord, the Committee recognised that the capital buffer related to credit risk implicitly covered other risks. The 'broad brush approach' in the 1988 Accord delivered an overall cushion of capital for both the measured risks (credit and market) and other (unmeasured) banking risks. To the extent that the new requirements for measured risks are a closer approximation to the actual level of those risks (as a result of the proposed changes to the credit risk calculation)—less of a buffer will exist for other risks. It should also be noted that banks themselves typically hold capital well in excess of the current regulatory minimum and that some are already allocating economic capital for other risks.

Events such as the September 11 terrorist attacks, rogue trading losses at Societe Generale, Barings, AIB, UBS and National Australia Bank serve to highlight the fact that the scope of risk management extends beyond merely market and credit risk. These reasons underscore banks' and supervisors' growing focus upon the identification and measurement of operational risk. The list of risks (and, more importantly, the scale of these risks) faced by banks today includes fraud, system failures, terrorism and employee compensation claims. These types of risk are generally classified under the term 'operational risks'.

The identification and measurement of operational risk is a

real and live issue for modern-day banks, particularly since the decision by the Basel Committee on Banking Supervision (BCBS) to introduce a capital charge for this risk as a part of the new capital adequacy framework (Basel III).

2.2 Emergence of Operational Risks

Banks and financial institutions are undergoing a sea change today and face an environment marked by growing consolidation, rising customer expectations, increasing regulatory requirements, proliferating financial engineering, uprising technological innovation and mounting competition. This has increased the probability of failure or mistakes from the operations point of view—resulting in an increased focus on managing operational risks.

Deregulation and globalisation of financial services, together with the growing sophistication of financial technology, are making the activities of banks and thus their profiles more complex. Evolving banking practices suggest that risks other than credit risks and market risks can be substantial. Examples of these new and growing risks faced by banks include the following.

If not properly controlled, the greater use of more highly automated technology has the potential to transform risks from manual processing errors to system failure risks, as greater reliance is placed on integrated systems. Emergence of e-commerce has brought with it, potential risks (e.g. internal and external fraud and system securities issues). Emergence of banks acting as very large volume service providers creates the need for continual maintenance of high-grade internal controls and back-up systems.

Growing use of outsourcing arrangements and the participation in clearing and settlement systems can mitigate some risks but can also present significant other risks to banks. Large-scale acquisitions, mergers, de-mergers and consolidations test the viability of new or newly integrated systems.

Banks may engage in risk mitigation techniques (e.g.

collateral, derivatives, netting arrangements and asset securitisations) to optimise their exposure to market risk and credit risk, but which in turn may produce other forms of risk (e.g. legal risk).

2.3 Operational Risk Defined

Operational risk is one area of risk that is faced by all organisations. More complex the organisation is, more exposed it would be to operational risk. Operational risk would arise due to deviations from normal and planned functioning of systems, procedures, and technology and human failures of omission and commission which impact revenues of an organisation adversely.

Operational risk is "the risk of a change in value caused by the fact that actual losses, incurred for inadequate or failed internal processes, people and systems, or from external events (including legal risk), differ from the expected losses". This definition from the Basel II regulations was also adopted by the European Union Solvency II Directive. In October 2014, the Basel Committee on Banking Supervision proposed a revision to its operational risk capital framework that sets out a new standardized approach to replace the basic indicator approach and the standardized approach for calculating operational risk capital.

It can also include other classes of risk, such as fraud, security, privacy protection, legal risks, physical (e.g. infrastructure shutdown) or environmental risks.

Operational risk is a broad discipline, close to good management and quality management. Operational risk is associated with human error, system failures and inadequate procedures and controls. It is the risk of loss arising from the potential that inadequate information system, technology failures, breaches in internal controls, fraud, unforeseen catastrophes, or other operational problems may result in unexpected losses or reputation problems. Operational risk exists in all products and business activities. In similar fashion, operational risks affect client satisfaction, reputation and shareholder value, all while increasing business volatility.

Contrary to other risks (e.g. credit risk, market risk, and insurance risk), operational risks are usually not willingly incurred nor are they revenue driven. Moreover, they are not diversifiable and cannot be laid off, meaning that, as long as people, systems and processes remain imperfect, operational risk cannot be fully eliminated. Operational risk is, nonetheless, manageable as to keep losses within some level of risk tolerance (i.e. the amount of risk one is prepared to accept in pursuit of his objectives), determined by balancing the costs of improvement against the expected benefits. Wider trends such as globalization, the expansion of the internet and the rise of social media, as well as the increasing demands for greater corporate accountability worldwide, reinforce the need for proper operational risk management.

The Basel II Committee defines operational risk as, "The risk of direct or indirect loss resulting from inadequate or failed internal processes, people and systems or from external events". The definition also includes legal risks resulting from regulatory actions and private settlements. Risks resulting from strategic business decisions and loss or damage of reputation are not included.

However, the Basel Committee recognizes that operational risk is a term that has a variety of meanings and therefore, for internal purposes, banks are permitted to adopt their own definitions of operational risk, provided that the minimum elements in the Committee's definition are included.

The Basel II definition of operational risk excludes, for example, strategic risk—the risk of a loss arising from a poor strategic business decision. Strategic and reputational risk is not included in this definition for the purpose of a minimum regulatory operational risk capital charge. This definition focuses on the causes of operational risk and the Committee believes that this is appropriate for both risk management and, ultimately, measurement. However, in reviewing the progress of the industry in the measurement of operational risk, the Committee is aware that causal measurement and modelling of operational risk remains at the earliest stages. For this reason, the Committee sets out further details on the effects of operational losses, in terms of loss types, to allow data collection and measurement to commence.

Other risk terms are seen as potential consequences of operational risk events. For example, reputational risk (damage to an organization through loss of its reputation or standing) can arise as a consequence (or impact) of operational failures—as well as from other events.

Impact of various forms of operational risk on the organisation may vary in degree i.e., some risks may have more potential of causing damages while some may have less potential, some may occur more frequently while some may occur less frequently. Thus, nature of operational risk may be:

- Operational risk exists almost everywhere in the organisation.
- Operational risks vary in their components. Some are high occurrence low value risks, while some are low occurrence high value risks.
- Operational risks in the organisation continuously change especially when an organisation is undergoing changes.

2.4 Classification of Operational Risks

The Second Consultative Paper of Basel II suggested classification of operational risks based on the 'Causes' and 'Effects'.

2.4.1 Cause-based Operational Risks:

- **People-oriented Causes:** Negligence, incompetence, insufficient training, integrity, key men.
- **Process-oriented (Operational Control Based) Causes:** Inadequate segregation of duties, lack of management supervision, inadequate procedures.
- **Process-oriented (Transaction Based) Causes:** Business volume fluctuation, organisational complexity, product

complexity and major changes.

- **Technology-oriented Causes:** Poor technology and telecom, obsolete applications, lack of automation, information system complexity, poor design, development and testing.
- **External Causes:** Natural disasters, operational failures of a third party, deteriorated social or political context.

2.4.2 Effect-based Operational Risks:

- Legal liability.
- Regulatory, compliance and taxation penalties.
- Loss or damage to assets.
- Restitution.
- Loss of recourse.
- Write-downs.

2.5 Forms of Operational Risks

A clear appreciation and understanding by banks of what is meant by operational risk is critical to the effective management and control of this risk category. It is also important to consider the full range of material operational risks facing a bank and capture all significant causes of severe operational losses. Operational risk is pervasive, complex and dynamic. Unlike market and credit risk, which tend to be in specific areas of business, operational risk is inherent in all business processes. Operational risk may manifest in a variety of ways in the banking industry.

The Basel Committee has identified the following types of operational risk events in the Third Consultative Paper as having the potential to result in substantial losses.

2.5.1 Internal Fraud: Losses due to acts of a type intended to commit fraud, misappropriate property or circumvent regulations, the law or company policy, excluding diversity/discrimination events, which involve at least one internal party. For example, intentional misreporting of positions, employee theft, and insider trading on an employee's own account.

2.5.2 External Fraud: Losses due to acts of a type intended to defraud, misappropriate property or circumvent the law, by a third party. For example, robbery, forgery, cheque kiting, and damage from computer hacking.

2.5.3 Employment Practices and Workplace Safety: Losses arising from acts inconsistent with employment, health or safety laws or agreements, from payment of personal injury claims, or from diversity/discrimination events, e.g. workers compensation claims, violation of employee health and safety rules, organised labour activities, discrimination claims, and general liability.

2.5.4 Clients, Products and Business Practices: Losses arising from an unintentional or negligent failure to meet a professional obligation to specific clients (including fiduciary and suitability requirements), or from the nature or design of a product. For example, fiduciary breaches, misuse of confidential customer information, improper trading activities on the bank's account, money laundering, and sale of unauthorised products.

2.5.5 Damage to Physical Assets: Losses arising from loss or damage to physical assets from natural disaster or other events. For example, terrorism, vandalism, earthquakes, fires and floods.

2.5.6 Business Disruption and System Failures: Losses arising from disruption of business or system failure. For example, hardware and software failures, telecommunication problems, and utility outages.

2.5.7 Execution, Delivery and Process Management: Losses from failed transaction processing or process management, from relations with trade counterparts and vendors. For example, data entry errors, collateral management failures, incomplete legal documentation, and unauthorized access given to client accounts, non-client counterparty mis-performance, and vendor disputes.

2.6 Relevance of Operational Risk Function

Growing number of high-profile operational loss events

worldwide have led banks and supervisors to increasingly view operational risk management as an integral part of risk management activity. Management of specific operational risks is not a new practice; it has always been important for banks to try to prevent fraud, maintain the integrity of internal controls, and reduce errors in transaction processing, and so on. However, what is relatively new is the view that operational risk management is a comprehensive practice comparable to the management of credit and market risks. The objective of operational risk management is the same as for credit, market and liquidity risks, i.e. to find out the extent of the financial institution's operational risk exposure; to understand what drives it, to allocate capital against it and identify trends internally and externally that would help predicting it.

The management of specific operational risks is not a new practice; it has always been important for banks to try to prevent fraud, maintain the integrity of internal controls, and reduce errors in transactions processing, and so on. Operational risk differs from other banking risks in that it is typically not directly taken in return for an expected reward but is implicit in the ordinary course of corporate activity and has the potential to affect the risk management process. However, it is recognised that in some business lines with minimal credit or market risks, the decision to incur operational risk or compete, based on the perceived ability to manage and effectively price this risk, is an integral part of a bank's risk/reward calculus. At the same time, failure to properly manage operational risk can result in a misstatement of an institution's risk profile and expose the institution to significant losses. Management of operational risk is taken to mean the identification, assessment and/or measurement, monitoring and control/mitigation of this risk.

2.7 Key Elements in Operational Risk Management

Operational risk management is at the core of a bank's

operations—integrating risk management practices into processes, systems and culture. As a pro-active partner to senior management, ORM's value lies in supporting and challenging them to align the business control environment with the bank's strategy by measuring and mitigating risk exposure and contributing to optimal return for stakeholders. For instance, HSBC has invested heavily in understanding customer behaviour through new systems initially designed for fraud detection, which is now being leveraged beyond compliance to address more effective customer service.

The ORM group of an organization keeps its people up-to-date on problems that have happened to other financial institutions, allowing it to take a more proactive approach. "*Our goal is for employees to look at ORM as a business stakeholder and a shareholder, involving them on all levels and bring stability into their jobs*", said the senior vice president of Operational and Compliance Risk Management Group. A noted financial services company, on the other hand, incorporates its ORM approach as an extension of its business line and not a separate entity. The company has implemented an operational risk umbrella that encompasses all aspects of potential risks—bank protection, fraud prevention, key risk indicators, capture of operational loss data, business line risk oversight and new products and initiatives for data security. Its chief risk officer quotes, "*We utilize our ORM practices to gain respect and appreciation of all our business lines by really understanding their issues, and being part of the overall solution*".

Thus, operational risk management framework is required which will depict the clear picture for this. It provides the strategic direction and ensures that an effective operational risk management and measurement process is adopted throughout the institution. Each institution's operational risk profile is unique and requires a tailored risk management approach appropriate for the scale and materiality of the risk present, and the size of the institution. There is no single framework that would suit every institution; different approaches will be needed for different institutions. In fact, many operational risk management techniques continue to evolve rapidly to keep pace with new technologies, business models and applications. Operation risk is more a risk management than measurement issue. The key elements in the operational risk management process include the following:

- Appropriate policies and procedures.
- Efforts to identify and measure operational risk.
- Effective monitoring and reporting.
- A sound system of internal controls.
- Appropriate testing and verification of the operational risk framework.

2.8 Monitoring of Operational Risks

An effective monitoring process is essential for adequately managing operational risk. Regular monitoring activities can offer the advantage of quickly detecting and correcting deficiencies in the policies, processes and procedures for managing operational risk. Promptly detecting and addressing these deficiencies can substantially reduce the potential frequency and/or severity of a loss. Banks should implement a process to regularly monitor operational risk profiles and material exposures to losses. In addition to monitoring operational loss events, banks should identify appropriate indicators that provide early warning of an increased risk of future losses. Such indicators (often referred to as early warning indicators) should be forward-looking and could reflect potential sources of operational risk such as rapid growth, the introduction of new products, employee turnover, transaction breaks, system downtime, and so on.

When thresholds are directly linked to these indicators, an effective monitoring process can help identify key material risks in a transparent manner and enable the bank to act upon these risks appropriately. The frequency of monitoring should reflect the risks involved and the frequency and nature of changes in the operating environment. Monitoring should be an integrated part of a bank's activities. The results of these monitoring activities should be included in regular management and board reports, as should compliance reviews performed by the internal audit and/or risk management functions. Management should establish a programme to:

- Monitor assessment of the exposure to all types of operational risks faced by the institution;
- Assess the quality and appropriateness of mitigating actions, including the extent to which identifiable risks can be transferred outside the institution; and
- Ensure that adequate controls and systems are in place to identify and address problems before they become major concerns.

Senior management should receive regular reports from appropriate areas such as business units, group functions, the operational risk management unit and internal audit. Reports should fully reflect any identified problem areas and should motivate timely corrective action on outstanding issues. To ensure the usefulness and reliability of these risk reports and audit reports, management should regularly verify the timeliness, accuracy, and relevance of reporting systems and internal controls in general. For the purpose of operational risk management, the activities of a bank may be mapped into eight business lines:

1. Corporate finance.
2. Trading and sales.
3. Retail banking.
4. Commercial banking.
5. Payment and settlement.
6. Agency services.
7. Asset management.
8. Retail brokerages.

2.9 Control/Mitigation of Operational Risks

Risk management is the process of mitigating the risks

faced by a bank. With regard to operational risk, several methods may be adopted for mitigating the risk. For example, losses that might arise on account of natural disasters can be insured against. Losses that might arise from business disruptions due to telecommunication or electrical failures can be mitigated by establishing redundant backup facilities. Loss due to internal factors, like employee fraud or product flaws, which may be difficult to identify and insure against, can be mitigated through strong internal auditing procedures. Both the board of directors and senior management are an integral part of the regular activities of a bank—since such integration enables quick responses to changing conditions and avoids unnecessary costs.

A system of effective internal control can help to ensure that the bank will comply with laws and regulations as well as policies, plans, internal rules and procedures, and decrease the risk of unexpected losses or damage to the bank's reputation. The internal control process, which historically has been a mechanism for reducing instances of fraud, misappropriation and errors, has become more extensive, addressing all the various risks faced by banking organisations. It is now recognised that a sound internal control process is critical to a bank's ability to meet its established goals, and to maintain its financial viability.

Internal audit is a part of the ongoing monitoring of the bank's system of internal controls and of its internal capital assessment procedure, because internal audit provides an independent assessment of the adequacy of, and compliance with, the bank's established policies and procedures. Banks should have policies, processes and procedures to control and/or mitigate material operational risks. Banks should periodically review their risk limitation and control strategies and should adjust their operational risk profile accordingly using appropriate strategies, in light of their overall risk appetite and profile.

2.10 Core Elements of Operational Risk Framework

There is no 'one-size-fits-all' approach to ORM—as every enterprise follows a framework that is specific to its own internal operating environment. When inquired about the standard ORM framework, a risk expert notes, "There is no 'standard' standard. Ultimately, the operational risk framework should not merely be Basel-compliant; it should also provide the bank with mechanisms for improving overall risk culture and behaviour towards operational risk management. Understanding our risks should lead to better decision-making and reflect in our performance". A robust operational risk management framework is made up of the following core components.

2.10.1 Governance: It is the process by which the board of directors define key objectives for the bank and oversee progress towards achieving those objectives. It defines overall operational risk culture in organization, and sets the tone as to how a bank implements and executes its operational risk management strategy. A successfully executed risk strategy often results in risk being firmly embedded in the vision, strategies, tools, and tactics of the organization. Governance sets the precedence for strategy, structure and execution.

2.10.2 Clear Strategy: A bank's strategy for operational risk drives the other components within the management framework and provides clear guidance on risk appetite or tolerance, policies, and processes for day-to-day risk management.

2.10.3 Appetite and Policy: An ideal risk management process ensures that organizational behaviour is driven by its risk appetite. Adopting an operational risk strategy aligned to risk appetite, leads to informed business and investment decisions.

2.10.4 Ensures Proper Communication: An organization's top management must identify, assess, decide, implement, audit and supervise their strategic risks. There should be a strategic policy at the board level to focus on managing risk at all levels and conscious efforts should be made to ensure that these policies are communicated at all levels and across the entire value chain.

2.10.5 Periodic Evaluation: An ideal risk management process puts improvement of risk performance on a competitive level with other important missions concerned—periodically evaluating the ORM performance goals in the light of internal and external factors. Depending upon the criticality of internal operating environment and key external factors, an organization must review the strategic policies inside out.

2.10.6 Structure: When designing the operational risk management structure, the bank's overall risk scenario should serve as a guideline. This includes initiatives like laying down a hierarchical structure that leverages current risk processes, developing risk measurement models to assess regulatory and economic capital, and allocating economic capital vis-à-vis the actual risk confronted. Centralized aggregation of operational risk information collected via various self-assessments across the organization, further provides useful insights for the desired hierarchical structure. The implementation of these concepts allows risk to be handled consistently throughout the organization.

2.10.7 Execution: Once operational risk management structure has been established by an organization, adequate procedures should be designed and implemented to ensure execution of and compliance with these policies at business line level. The first step includes identification and assessment of operational risk inherent in day-to-day processes of the bank. After assessment of inherent risk, target tolerance limit of risk should be established. This is commonly accomplished by calculating the probability/likelihood of materialization of risk, by considering the drivers or causes of the risk together with the assessment of its impact. The results of the risk assessment and quantification process enables management to compare the risks with its operational risk strategy and policies, identify those risk exposures that are unacceptable to the institution or are outside the institution's risk appetite, and select and prioritise appropriate mechanisms for mitigation.

Finally, appropriate risk mitigation and internal control procedures are established by the business units so that the residual risk is mitigated to the acceptable level. Regular reviews must be carried out, to analyse the control environment and test the effectiveness of implemented controls, thereby ensuring that the business operations are conducted within acceptable risk limits. Further, it is essential that the top management ensures consistent monitoring and controlling of operational risk, and that risk information is received by the appropriate people, on a timely basis, in a form and format that will aid in monitoring and control. Operational risk metrics or 'key risk indicators' (KRIs) are established to ensure that timely warning is received prior to the occurrence of an event. Key to effective KRIs lies in setting threshold at the acceptable level of risk. Execution and implementation of operational risk framework is a key to setting up an effective operational risk environment ensuring that business is conducted within appropriate risk tolerance limit.

2.11 Operational Risk Management in Indian Banks

The Reserve Bank of India is the regulator and supervisor of the banking system in India and is entrusted with the task of framing the capital adequacy guidelines for banks in India under Basel II. Public sector banks, where the Government of India is a major shareholder, dominate the Indian banking system, accounting for nearly three-fourths of total assets and income. These banks are large and very old banks, operating through thousands of branches spread all over the country. The new private sector banks are fully automated from day one and operate like other high-tech foreign banks. The private sector banks have grown rapidly since the onset of reforms and have increased their share in total assets of the banking industry, whereas the public sector banks have witnessed shrinkage in their market share.

The public sector banks have only recently started automating their processes and operations. This transition has posed significant challenges in the management of operational risk to the banks as introduction of new technology and complete overhauling of the existing systems requires a re-engineering of business processes, training of manpower, audit in a computerized environment and other related operational risk challenges. The new generation private sector banks on the other hand have to deal with the risks arising from growth at a scorching pace. With the reforms in the Indian banking sector and banks being allowed to access new markets and sophisticated products, the Reserve Bank of India has also been repeatedly advising the banks to have in place an effective and resilient control framework in place to manage operational risks.

Specific guidance on management of operational risks has also been issued as per which some banks; especially the larger and internationally active banks are expected to move along the range towards more sophisticated approaches as they develop more sophisticated operational risk management systems and practices which meet the prescribed qualifying criteria. Therefore, we can say that the discipline of operational risk is at a crossroads. Despite the efforts to control operational risk, banks still have much work to do? For this, they have to face the following challenges of managing the operational risk.

2.11.1 Increased Costs of Compliance: Development of an ORM model as part of a regulatory and economic capital framework is complex and takes time. There is a general agreement that the major ORM challenge is escalating cost of compliance.

2.11.2 Improper Measurement of Operational Risk: Many enterprises hold that their institutions are measuring operational risk. However, very few of them have been able to complete the Basel II quantification requirements, or yet to formalize the measurement process around the Basel II framework.

2.11.3 Access to Appropriate Information and Reporting: Effective management of operational risk requires diverse information from a variety of sources—including, for example, risk reports, risk and control profiles, operational risk incidents, key risk indicators, risk heat maps, and rules and definitions—for regulatory, capital and economic capital reporting.

2.11.4 Development of Business Line Databases: A well-structured operational risk framework requires development of business-line databases to capture loss events attributable to various categories of operational risk. Basel II specifically requires a minimum of three years of data for initial implementation and ultimately five years for the advanced measurement approaches (AMA). The need for historical data (including external data) has been a cause for concern for many enterprises.

2.11.5 Implementing ORM Systems: Amid regulatory efforts to revamp the bank's immunity to operational risk, and its implications on efficient financial intermediation, many organizations are looking to go beyond traditional approaches and implement a consolidated ORM framework across entire value chain. Development of an ORM model as part of a regulatory and economic capital framework, however, is complex and takes time. Some banks may either still be struggling with the requirements of the 'Sound Practices for ORM', BIS paper, which spells out how to introduce ORM principles, may not yet have in place the required governance or framework. Factors like lack of understanding of upcoming technology regarding operational risk management, failure to get the top management to focus on the benefits of the programme, improved productivity and quality, as well as on loss reduction, and lack of meaningful and timely data across business units and product lines, makes the implementation of an ORM system, all the more formidable.

2.11.6 Tone at the Top: Effective risk management programme starts with 'The Tone at the Top'—driven by the top management and adhered by the bottom line. However, if bank's top leaders perceive operational risk management solely as a regulatory mandate, rather than as an important means of enhancing competitiveness and performance, they may tend to be less supportive of such efforts. Management and the board must understand the importance of operational risk, demonstrate their support for its management, and designate an appropriate managing entity and framework—one that is a part of the bank's overall corporate governance framework.

By adopting an integrated operational risk framework, companies can ensure that all operational risk management initiatives are sustained and are aligned with the corporate strategy.

3

Risk Management in Banking Business

3.1 History of Indian Banking

The banking industry in India has a huge canvas of history, which covers the traditional banking practices from the time of British Government to the reforms period, nationalization to privatization of banks and now increasing numbers of foreign banks in India. Therefore, banking in India has been through a long journey. Banking industry in India has also achieved a new height with the changing times. The use of technology has brought a revolution in the working style of the banks. Nevertheless, the fundamental aspects of banking i.e. trust and the confidence of the people on the institution remain the same. The majority of the banks are still successful in keeping with the confidence of the shareholders as well as other stakeholders. However, the changing dynamics of banking business has brought new kinds of risk exposure.

The financial sector in various economies—like that of India—is undergoing a monumental change, factoring into account world events such as the 'banking crisis' across the globe a few years back. The various aspects of increasing global competition to Indian banks by foreign banks, increased deregulation, introduction of innovative products and financial instruments as well as innovation in delivery channels, have highlighted the need for Indian banks to be prepared in terms of risk management. Indian banks have been making great advancements in terms of technology, quality, as well as stability such that they have started to expand and diversify at a rapid rate.

However, such expansion brings these banks into the context of risk, especially with the onset of increased globalization and liberalization. In banks and other financial institutions, risk plays a major part in the earnings of a bank. The higher the risk, the higher the return, hence, it is essential to maintain a parity between risk and the return. Hence, management of credit risk, incorporating a set systematic and professional methods especially those defined by the Basel II, becomes an essential requirement of banks. The more risk averse a bank is, the safer is their capital base.

In the process of providing financial services (including agency and advisory activities), banks assume various kinds of financial risks. Over the last decade, an understanding of the place of commercial banks within the financial sector has improved substantially. There are activities performed by banks which do not have direct balance sheet implications.

3.2 Role of Banking Sector

Presently, the Indian economy is in the process of becoming a world class economy. The Indian banking industry is making great advancements in terms of quality, quantity, expansion and diversification and is keeping up with the updated technology, ability, stability and thrust of a financial system, where the commercial banks play a very important role. This emphasizes the special need for a strong and effective control system with extra concern for the risk involved in the business. Globalization, liberalization and privatization have opened up new methods of financial transactions where risk level is very high. In banks and financial institutions, risk is considered to be the most important factor of earnings. Therefore, they have to balance the relationship between risk and the return.

Banks and banking activities have evolved significantly over time with the introduction of financial services like deposit taking, lending money, currency exchange and money transfers. Because of the central role of money, banks had and still have an important role in the economy. Banks act as brokers between supply and demand of securities, and they transform short-term deposits into medium- and long-term credits. Specialized information on financial products is gathered by banks to improve investment decisions and to manage the risk. Like any other firm, banks are exposed to classical operational risks like infrastructure breakdown, supply problems, environmental risks etc.

More typical and important for a bank are the financial risks it takes by its transformation and brokerage function. A bank raises funds by attracting deposits, borrowing on the inter-bank market or issuing debt instruments in the financial market. Essentially, the bank's main activity is to buy and sell financial products with different profit and risk characteristics. This transformation from supply to demand side is not without risk. Banks are exposed to credit, market, operational, interest rate and liquidity risks. The appropriate management of these risks is a key issue to reduce the earnings' risk of a bank, and to reduce the risk of a bank becoming insolvent and that depositors' cannot be refunded.

Banks are firms that efficiently provide a wide range of financial services for profit. Not surprisingly, banks have an important role in the economy and the society as a whole. Their central role is to make the community's surplus of deposits and investments useful, by lending it to people for various investment purposes, like company growth, education, housing etc. Banks have a main role as financial intermediaries that provide a steady flow of funds from savers to borrowers and users. They generate profits from transaction fees on financial services and interest charges for lending, which correspond to two of their main functions as financial intermediaries. Banks have also started to provide additional services apart from deposit taking, lending, stock broking, money transactions and payment systems with the aim to make additional profits from cross-selling, e.g., insurance and investment products.

3.2.1 Brokerage Function: In the brokerage function, banks act as an agent or intermediary in a financial transaction, e.g., in the stock or bond market. The broker can represent a buyer or a seller of a financial asset, and buys or sells on behalf of the customer. In most cases, the broker asks for a fee in exchange of its services. This fee can be a fixed or percentage-based commission, or a combination of both.

3.2.2 Asset Transformation Function: The asset transformation function translates the product specifications requested by the savers to products requested by the borrowers. Savers, e.g. retail deposit savers, are more attracted by products with lower price risk, liquidity costs and monitoring costs. Borrowers, e.g., large corporations are more interested in long-term debt but carry a higher risk, i.e. the uncertainty about their pay back of the debt. Banks transform the safe, short-term and liquid small amounts of savings deposits to risky long-term debt to firms or firm borrowers. Banks have a sufficient number of risk experts to analyse the risk profile of the borrowers.

In their role as a financial intermediary, banks reduce market deficiencies on three domains.

3.2.3 Liquidity Intermediation: The bank matches the objectives of two main groups in the economy viz. consumers and investors. Consumers and household savers have a short-term horizon on which they want to optimize their utility function. Consumers prefer a smooth consumption pattern to minimize changes in utility and hold liquid reserves to absorb temporary shocks in purchasing power, e.g. due to unemployment or unexpected expenses (e.g. a broken car). Investors need long-term financing for long-term projects and may have short-term cash difficulties. This financing bears a higher risk. Such loans or debt is illiquid for whosoever provides it. Banks provide savings account deposits that provide a liquidity insurance for the consumers. The cost of the liquidity premium is covered by reduced interest rate. At the same time, banks use the savings deposits to provide for long-term illiquid investments. This is possible when the amount of deposits a bank holds is sufficiently stable over time by the law of large numbers.

3.2.4 Risk Intermediation: Banks provide low-risk saving deposit products to consumer and invest their deposits in more risky debt and other assets. This is possible by a good risk management and sufficient diversification. Banks hold sufficiently diversified portfolios in which the risk of an individual loan is reduced.

Not all loans will default at the same time. In general, banks transform different types of risk (credit, market, exchange rate, interest rate risk) and repackage it into an appropriate product for all economic agents. Another example is the securitization activity, where a risky portfolio is structured into various products with specific risk profiles tailored to the needs of different economic agents.

3.2.5 Information Intermediation: Information gathering is important to avoid economic pitfalls due to asymmetric information. Firm entrepreneurs are typically much better informed than the consumer savers. Such information asymmetry may have adverse impacts on the economy, known as the moral hazard and adverse selection problem.

In reality, we can say that management of financial institution is nothing but a management of risk. Managing financial risk systematically and professionally becomes an even more important task. Rising global competition, increasing deregulation, introduction of innovative products and delivery channels have pushed risk management to the forefront of today's financial landscape. Ability to gauge the risks and take appropriate position will be the key to success. It can be said that risk takers will survive, effective risk managers will prosper and risk averse are likely to perish. The risk arises due to uncertainties, which in turn arise due to changes taking place in prevailing economic, social and political environment and lack of non-availability of information concerning such changes. Risk is an exposure to a transaction with loss, which occurs with some probability and which can be expected, measured and minimized. In financial institutions, risk results from variations and fluctuations in assets or liability or both in income from assets or payments and on liabilities or in outflows and inflows of cash. Today, banks are facing various types of risks that financial intermediaries are exposed to, in the course of their business.

3.3 Deregulation of the Banking Sector

In India, banking sector has an important role to play for the overall development of an economy. It is the key driver of economic growth of the country and has a dynamic role to play in converting the idle capital resources for their optimum utilisation so as to attain maximum productivity. In fact, the foundation of a sound economy depends on how sound the banking sector is and vice-versa.

The banking sector is considerably strong at present but at the same time, banking is considered to be a very risky business. Because banking business lines are many and varied, commercial banking, corporate finance, trading and investment banking, retail banking and various financial services form the main business line of banks.

Financial institutions must take risk, but they must do so consciously. However, it should be borne in mind that banks are very fragile institutions which are built on customers' trust, brand reputation and above all, dangerous leverage. In case something goes wrong, banks can collapse and failure of one bank is sufficient to send shock waves right through the economy.

The Indian banking industry is making great strides in terms of quality, quantity, expansion and diversification and is keeping up with the updated technology. The ability, stability and thrust of a financial system, where the commercial banks play a very important role, emphasizes the need for a strong and effective control system with extra concern for the risk involved in the business.

Rising global competition, increasing deregulation, introduction of innovative products and delivery channels have pushed risk management to the forefront of today's financial landscape. Ability to gauge the risks and take appropriate position will be the key to success. Therefore, bank managements' must take utmost care in identifying the type as well as the degree of its risk exposure and tackle those effectively. Moreover, bankers must seè risk management as an ongoing and valued activity.

In other words, due to liberalisation, globalization and privatization, Indian banking system is in fierce competition not only from the domestic banks but from foreign banks alike and new methods of financial transaction have opened up where risk level is very high. Even disintermediation and deregulated environment has brought pressure on bank management in maintaining a good balance sheet amongst profitability, long-term viability etc.

Risk is inherent in any walk of life in general and in financial sector in particular. Till recently, due to regulated environment, banks could not afford to take risks. But of late, banks are exposed to some competition and hence are compelled to encounter various types of financial and non-financial risks.

Risks and uncertainties form an integral part of banking which by nature entails taking risks. Therefore, they have to balance the relationship between risk and the return. In reality, we can say that management of financial institution is nothing but a management of risk.

In short, the two most important developments that have made it imperative for Indian commercial banks to give more emphasis on risk management are as under:

- **Deregulation**: The era of financial sector reforms which started in early 1990s has culminated in deregulation in a phased manner. Deregulation has given banks more autonomy in areas like lending, investment, interest rate structure etc. As a result of these developments, banks are required to manage their own business themselves and at the same time maintain liquidity and profitability. This has made it imperative for banks to pay more attention to risk management.
- **Technological Innovations**: Technological innovations

have provided a platform to the banks for creating an environment for efficient customer services as also for designing new products. In fact, it is the technological innovation that has helped banks to manage the assets and liabilities in a better way, providing various delivery channels, reducing processing time of transactions and reducing manual intervention in back office functions etc. However, all these developments have also increased the diversity and complexity of risks, which need to be managed professionally so that the opportunities provided by the technology are not negated.

3.4 What Kinds of Risks Are Being Absorbed?

The risks contained in the bank's principle activities, i.e., those involving its own balance sheet and its basic business of lending and borrowing, are not all borne by the bank itself. In many instances, the institution will eliminate or mitigate the financial risk associated with a transaction by proper business practices; in others, it will shift the risk to other parties through a combination of pricing and product design.

The banking industry recognizes that an institution need not engage in business in a manner that unnecessarily imposes risk upon it; nor should it absorb risk that can be efficiently transferred to other participants. Rather, it should only manage risks at the firm level that are more efficiently managed there than by the market itself or by their owners in their own portfolios. In short, it should accept only those risks that are uniquely a part of the bank's array of services.

Elsewhere, Oldfield and Santomero (1997) argued that risks facing all financial institutions can be segmented into three separable types, from a management perspective. These are as under:

- Risks that can be eliminated or avoided by simple business practices.
- Risks that can be transferred to other participants.
- Risks that must be actively managed at the firm level.

In the first of these cases, the practice of risk avoidance involves actions to reduce the chances of idiosyncratic losses from standard banking activity by eliminating risks that are superfluous to the institution's business purpose. Common risk avoidance practices here include at least three types of actions. The standardization of process, contracts and procedures to prevent inefficient or incorrect financial decisions is the first of these. The construction of portfolios that benefit from diversification across borrowers and that reduce the effects of any one loss experience is another. Finally, the implementation of incentive-compatible contracts with the institution's management to require that employees be held accountable is the third. In each case the goal is to rid the firm of risks that are not essential to the financial service provided, or to absorb only an optimal quantity of a particular kind of risk.

There are also some risks that can be eliminated, or at least substantially reduced through the technique of risk transfer. Markets exist for many of the risks borne by the banking firm. Interest rate risk can be transferred by interest rate products such as swaps or other derivatives. Borrowing terms can be altered to effect a change in their duration. Finally, the bank can buy or sell financial claims to diversify or concentrate the risks that result in from servicing its client base. To the extent that the financial risks of the assets created by the firm are understood by the market, these assets can be sold at their fair value. Unless the institution has a comparative advantage in managing the attendant risk and/or a desire for the embedded risk they contain, there is no reason for the bank to absorb such risks, rather than transfer them.

However, there are two classes of assets or activities where the risk inherent in the activity must and should be absorbed at the bank level. In these cases, good reasons exist for using firm resources to manage bank level risk. The first of these includes financial assets or activities where the nature of the embedded risk may be complex and difficult to communicate to third parties. This is the case when the bank holds complex and proprietary assets that have thin, if not non-existent, secondary markets. Communication in such cases may be more difficult or expensive than hedging the underlying risk.

Moreover, revealing information about the customer may give competitors an undue advantage. The second case included proprietary positions that are accepted because of their risks, and their expected return. Here, risk positions that are central to the bank's business purpose are absorbed. Credit risk inherent in the lending activity is a clear case in point, as is market risk for the trading desk of banks active in certain markets. In all such circumstances, risk is absorbed and needs to be monitored and managed efficiently by the institution. Only then will the firm systematically achieve its financial performance goal.

The key driver in managing all the business lines includes enhancing risk adjusted expected return. This is the common factor for all the business lines. From the risk management point of view, banking business lines may be grouped broadly into major heads which are:

- The banking book.
- The trading portfolio.
- Off-balance sheet exposures.

3.4.1 Banking Book: The banking book is an accounting term that refers to assets in a bank's balance sheet that are expected to be held till maturity. Banks are not required to mark these to market. Unless there is reason to believe that the counterparty will default on its obligation, they are held at historical cost. The banking book includes all advances, deposits and borrowings, which usually arise from commercial and retail banking operations. All assets and liabilities in banking book have the following characteristics:

- They are normally held until maturity; and
- Accrual system of accounting is applied.

Since all assets and liabilities in the banking book are held until maturity, maturity mismatch between assets and liabilities result in excess or shortage of liquidity. This is commonly known as 'liquidity risk'. In addition, when interest rate changes take place during the period, such assets and liabilities are held in the banking book. Therefore, interest rates on assets as well as liabilities change on their maturity. This affects net interest margin, i.e., interest received net of interest paid. Further, the asset side of the banking book generates credit risk arising from defaults in payments of principal and/or interest by the borrowers. This is called 'default risk' or 'credit risk'. Since banking book is not open to market, it is not exposed to market risk as well. In addition to all these risks, exposures under banking book suffer from what is termed as 'operational risk'. Hence, the banking book is mainly exposed to liquidity risk, interest rate risk, default or credit risk and operational risks.

3.4.2 Trading Book: The trading book is an accounting term that refers to assets held by a bank that are regularly traded. The trading book is required under Basel II and III to be marked to market daily. The value-at-risk for assets in the trading book is measured on a ten-day time horizon under Basel II. If a client wishes to sell debt securities to a bank instead of taking a loan, the asset will be assigned to the trading book instead. The bank will then keep specific risk capital for the securities as well as for the market risk capital. The trading book includes all assets that are marketable, i.e., they can be traded in the market. The features of trading book assets are as under:

- They are normally not held until maturity and positions are liquidated in the market after holding it for a period.
- Mark-to-market system is followed and the difference between market price and book value is taken to profit and loss account.

Trading book mostly comprises of fixed income securities, equities, foreign exchange holdings, commodities, etc., held by the bank on its own account. Trading book is exposed to market risk including credit risk, liquidation risk and operational risk.

The main differences between the two are: (a) assets that are held for trading are put in the trading book, assets that are held to maturity are held in the banking book; (b) assets in the trading book are marked-to-market daily and assets in the banking book are held at historic cost; (c) the value-at-risk for assets in the trading book is calculated at a 99 percent confidence level based on a 10-day time horizon. The value-at-risk for assets in the banking books are calculated at a 99.9 percent confidence level on a one-year horizon.

3.4.3 Off-balance Sheet Exposures: Off-balance sheet exposures are contingent in nature. These contingencies adversely affect the revenue generation of banks. Banks may also have contingency receivables.

Here, banks are the beneficiaries, subject to certain contingencies. Derivatives are off-balance sheet market exposures. They may be swaps, futures, forward contracts, foreign currency contracts, options etc. Contingent exposure may become a fund-based exposure.

Such exposures may become a part of the banking book or trading book, depending on the nature of the off-balance sheet exposure. Therefore, off-balance sheet exposures may include liquidity risk, interest rate risk, default or credit risk and operational risk.

3.5 Types of Risks Banks Face

Banks that manage their risks have a competitive advantage. They take risks consciously, anticipate adverse changes and protect themselves from such changes. In view of growing complexity of banks' business and the dynamic operating environment, risk management has become very significant, especially in the financial sector. As stated earlier, the term *risk* and the types associated to it would refer to mean financial risk or uncertainty of financial loss. If we consider risk in terms of probability of occurrence frequently, we measure risk on a scale, with certainty of occurrence at one end and certainty of non-occurrence at the other end. Risk is the greatest where the probability of occurrence or non-occurrence is equal.

Risk at the apex level may be visualized as the probability of a bank's financial health being impaired due to one or more contingent factors. While the parameters indicating the banks' health may vary from net interest margin to market value of equity, the factor which can cause hurt the most are also numerous.

For instance, there could be default in repayment of loans by borrowers or change in value of assets or disruption of operation due to reason like technological failure. These factors may be classified as credit risk and market risk.

The Reserve Bank of India guidelines issued in October 1999 has identified and categorized the majority of risk into three major categories assumed to be encountered by banks and these are credit risk, market risk and operational risk.

The types of risks can be fundamentally sub-divided in two categories, i.e. financial and non-financial risk. Financial risks would involve all those aspects which deal mainly with financial aspects of the bank. These can be further sub-divided into credit risk and market risk. Both credit and market risk may be further sub-divided.

Non-financial risks would entail all the risks faced by the banks in their regular workings, i.e. operational risk, strategic risk, funding risk, political risk and legal risk.

Non-financial risk refers to those risks that may affect a bank's business growth, marketability of its product and services, likely failure of its strategies aimed at business growth etc. These risks may arise on account of management failures, competition, non-availability of suitable products/services, external factors etc.

Thus, the risks to which a bank is particularly exposed in its operations are: liquidity risk, credit risk, market risks (interest rate risk, foreign exchange risk and risk from change in market price of securities, financial derivatives and commodities), exposure risks, investment risks, risks relating to the country of origin of the entity to which a bank is exposed, operational risk, legal risk, reputational risk and strategic risk.

3.5.1 Liquidity Risk: Bank deposits generally have a much shorter contractual maturity than loans and liquidity management needs to provide a cushion to cover anticipated deposit withdrawals. Liquidity is the ability to efficiently accommodate deposit as also reduction in liabilities and to fund the loan growth and possible funding of the off-balance sheet claims. The cash flows are placed in different time buckets based on future likely behaviour of assets, liabilities and off-balance sheet items.

Liquidity of bank may be defined as the ability to meet anticipated and contingent cash needs. Cash needs arise from withdrawal of deposits, liability maturities and loan disbursals. The requirement for cash is met by increases in deposits and borrowings, loan repayments, investment maturities and the sale of assets. Inadequate liquidity can lead to unexpected cash shortfalls that must be covered at inordinate cost which reduces profitability. It can lead to liquidity insolvency of the bank without being capital insolvent.

Hence, liquidity is a bank's capacity to fund increase in assets and meet both expected and unexpected cash and collateral obligations at reasonable cost and without incurring unacceptable losses. Liquidity risk is the inability of a bank to meet such obligations as they become due, without adversely affecting the bank's financial condition. Effective liquidity risk management helps ensure a bank's ability to meet its obligations as they fall due and reduces the probability of an adverse situation developing. This assumes significance on account of the fact that liquidity crisis, even at a single institution, can have systemic implications.

Traditionally, liquidity has been defined as the capacity of financial institutions to finance increase in their assets and comply with their liabilities as these mature. Bank liquidity has two distinct but interrelated dimensions: liability (or cash) liquidity, which refers to the ability to obtain funding in the market and asset (or market) liquidity, associated with the possibility of selling the assets. Both concepts are interrelated, and the interaction between them tends towards their mutual reinforcement. The liquidity risk of banks arises from funding of long-term assets by short-term liabilities, thereby making the liabilities subject to rollover or refinancing risk. Liquidity risk is usually of an individual nature, but in certain situations may compromise the liquidity of the financial system. Thus, it is the risk of negative effects on the financial result and capital of the bank caused by the bank's inability to meet all its due obligations.

Liquidity risk consists of funding risk, time risk and call risk. These are discussed below.

3.5.2 Funding Risk: Funding liquidity risk is defined as the inability to obtain funds to meet cash flow obligations. For banks, funding liquidity risk is crucial. This arises from the need to replace net outflows due to unanticipated withdrawal/non-renewal of deposits (wholesale and retail). Funding liquidity risk is the risk that a bank will not be able to meet efficiently due to the expected and unexpected current and future cash flows and collateral needs, without affecting either its daily operations or its financial condition.

3.5.3 Credit Risk: The field of credit risk gained considerable momentum due to the increased competition in the field and the challenges of the present financial crisis. Credit risk is one of the main risks of commercial banks that will affect the banks' ability of sustainable operations. Credit risk is inherent to the business of lending funds to the operations linked closely to market risk variables. It is the risk of loss which arises if customers and counterparties cannot meet their payment obligations. Credit risk is the risk of loss due to default by a counter party in its contractual obligations, or as a result of reduction in the credit quality of the counter party. Credit risk is the risk of negative effects on the financial result and capital of the bank caused by borrower's default in its obligations to the bank.

Credit risk refers to the risk that a borrower will default on any type of debt by failing to make the required payments. The risk is primarily that of the lender and includes lost principal and interest, disruption to cash flows and increased collection cost. It the possibility of losses associated with decrease in the credit quality of the borrower or the counter parties. In the bank's portfolio, losses stem from outside default due to inability or unwillingness of the customer or the counter party to meet the commitments; losses may also result from reduction in the portfolio value arising from actual or perceived deterioration in credit quality.

The Basel Committee on Banking Supervision (BCBS) defines credit risk as the potential risk in which a bank borrower, or counter party, will fail to meet its payment obligations regarding the terms agreed with the bank. It includes both uncertainty involved in repayment of the bank's dues and repayment of dues on time. All banks face this type of risk. There is always scope for the borrower to default from his commitments for one or the other reason resulting in crystallization of credit risk to the bank. These losses could take the form of outright default or alternatively, losses from changes in portfolio value arising from actual or perceived deterioration in credit quality that is short of default. For most banks, loans are the largest and most obvious source of credit risk.

Generally, a financial institution's credit risk is not increased by the mere fact that a loan originated through an e-banking channel. However, management should consider additional precautions when originating and approving loans electronically, including assuring that the management information systems effectively track the performance of portfolios originating through e-banking channels. If not properly managed, these aspects can significantly increase the credit risk.

Thus, it is the most significant risk, more so in the Indian scenario, where the NPA level of the banking system is significantly high. The Asian financial crisis, which emerged due to rise in NPAs to over 30 percent of the total assets of the financial system of Indonesia, Malaysia, South Korea and Thailand, highlights the importance of management of credit risk The objective of credit risk management is to minimize the risk and maximize bank's risk adjusted rate of return by assuming and maintaining credit exposure within the acceptable parameters.

3.5.4 Market Risk: Market risk may be defined as the possibility of loss to bank caused by the changes in the market variables. It is the risk due to which the value of on-/off-balance sheet positions will be adversely affected by movements in equity and interest rate markets, currency exchange rates and commodity prices. Market risk is the risk to the bank's earnings and capital due to changes in the market level of interest rates or prices of securities, foreign exchange and equities, as well as because of the volatilities in those prices. Market risk is the risk of incurring losses in positions arising from movements in market prices on all positions held by the banks. Market risk is the risk of adverse deviations of the mark-to-market value of the trading portfolio, due to market movements, during the period of holding. This results from adverse movements of the market prices of interest rate instrument, equities and currencies. Market risk is also referred as 'price risk'. Price risk occurs when assets are sold before their stated maturities. The price risk is closely associated with the trading book, which is created for making profit out of short-term movements in interest rates.

Bank for International Settlement (BIS) defines market risk as, "the risk of losses in on- and off-balance sheet positions arising from movements in market prices". In this respect, the main factors contributing to market risk are equity, interest rate, foreign exchange and commodity risk. The total market risk is the aggregation of all the risk factors. Market risk can impact a company's business in many different ways. Exposure to market risk may arise as a result of the bank taking deliberate speculative positions or may come from the bank's market-making dealer activities.

For example, operating margins can be eroded due to the rising prices of raw materials or depreciating currencies in countries in which a company has foreign sales (direct market risk impact).

Changes in the market environment may eventually force companies to adjust the prices of their products or services, potentially altering sales volumes or competitiveness, depending on the positioning and market exposure of the company's competitors (the indirect impact of market risk on business results).

Some organizations may be paid to take market risks (e.g., financial organizations), but most seek to manage the impact of market risk on financial results.

The term market risk applies to: (i) that part of IRR which affects the price of interest rate instruments, (ii) pricing risk for all other assets/portfolio including commodities like gold that is held in the trading book of the bank, and (iii) foreign currency risk.

Foreign exchange risk also known as currency risk is a financial risk that exists when a financial transaction is denominated in a currency other than that of the base currency of the company. Foreign exchange risk also exists when the foreign subsidiary of a firm maintains financial statements in a currency other than the reporting currency of the consolidated entity. The risk is that there may be an adverse movement in the exchange rate of the denomination currency in relation to the base currency before the date when the transaction is completed. Investors and businesses exporting or importing goods and services or making foreign investments have an exchange rate risk which can have severe financial consequences; but steps can be taken to manage (i.e. reduce) the risk.

The risk inherent in running open foreign exchange positions have heightened in recent years by the pronounced volatility in forex rates, thereby adding a new dimension to the risk profile of banks' balance sheets.

Foreign exchange risk is the risk that a bank may suffer as a result of adverse exchange rate movement during a period in which it has an open position, either spot or forward or both in same foreign currency. Even in case where spot or forward positions in individual currencies are balanced, the maturity pattern of forward transactions may produce mismatches. There is also a settlement risk arising out of default of the counter party and out of time lag in settlement of one currency in one centre and the settlement of another currency in another time zone. Banks are also exposed to interest rate risk, which arises from the maturity mismatch of foreign currency position.

In the forex business, banks also face the risk of default of the counter parties (settlement risk). While such type of risk crystallisation does not cause principal loss, banks may have to undertake fresh transactions in the cash/spot market for replacing the failed transactions. Thus, banks may incur replacement cost, which depends upon the currency rate movements. Banks also face another risk called time-zone risk or Herstatt risk which arises out of time-lags in settlement of one currency in one centre and the settlement of another currency in another time zone. The forex transactions with counter parties from another country also trigger sovereign or country risk.

3.5.5 Interest Rate Risk: Interest rate risk arises when the net interest margin or the market value of equity (MVE) of an institution is affected due to changes in the interest rates. Interest rate risk is the potential negative impact on the net interest income and it refers to the vulnerability of an institution's financial condition to the movement in interest rates. In other words, interest rate risk is the risk of negative effects on the financial result and capital of the bank caused by changes in interest rates.

Changes in interest rate affect earnings, value of assets,

liability off-balance sheet items and cash flow. Earnings perspective involves analysing the impact of changes in interest rates on accrual or reported earnings in the near term. This is measured by measuring the changes in the net interest income (NII) equivalent to the difference between total interest income and total interest expense.

Net interest income, the difference between interest income and interest expense, is the main determinant of the profitability of banks. It is determined by interest rates on assets and paid for funds, volume of funds, and as a consequence, the changes in interest rate affect the net interest income.

Therefore, the objective of interest rate risk management is to maintain earnings, improve the capability and the ability to absorb potential loss and to ensure the adequacy of the compensation received for the risk taken and the effects of risk return trade-off.

IRR can be viewed in two ways—its impact on the earnings of the bank or its impact on the economic value of the bank's assets, liabilities and off-balance sheet (OBS) positions.

3.5.6 Operational Risk: Operational risk arises from fraud, processing errors, system disruptions or other unanticipated events resulting in the institutions' inability to deliver products or services. Strategic risk and reputation risk are not a part of operational risk. Operational risk is by itself not a new concept, it has by far not received the same amount of attention as credit and market risk, until recent years. Operational risk becomes a major constraint since it involves taking appropriate measures to ensure the qualitative transactions without processing errors in order to deliver the best services to the customers. Fundamental changes in financial markets, increasing globalization and deregulation, as well as corporate restructuring had a large impact on the magnitude and nature of operational risks confronting banks.

Always banks live with the risks arising out of human error, financial fraud and natural disasters. The recent happenings such as WTC tragedy, Barings debacle etc. has highlighted the potential losses on account of operational risk. Exponential growth in the use of technology and increase in global financial inter-linkages are the two primary changes that contributed to such risks. Operational risk, though defined as any risk that is not categorized as market or credit risk, is the risk of loss arising from inadequate or failed internal processes, people and systems or from external events. In order to mitigate this, internal control and internal audit systems are used as the primary means. Risk education for familiarizing the complex operations at all levels of staff can also reduce operational risk. Insurance cover is one of the important mitigators of operational risk. Operational risk events are associated with weak links in internal control procedures. The key to management of operational risk lies in the bank's ability to assess its process for vulnerability and establish controls as well as safeguards, while providing for unanticipated worst-case scenarios.

Operational risk is the risk of negative effects on the financial result and capital of the bank caused by omissions in the work of employees, inadequate internal procedures and processes, inadequate management of information and other systems, and unforeseeable external events.

In other words, it may be defined as the risk of loss resulting from inadequate or failed internal process, people and systems or because of external events.

Operational risk is "the risk of a change in value caused by the fact that actual losses, incurred for inadequate or failed internal processes, people and systems, or from external events (including legal risk), differ from the expected losses". This definition from the Basel II regulations was also adopted by the European Union Solvency II Directive. It can also include other classes of risk, such as fraud, security, privacy protection, legal risks, physical (e.g. infrastructure shutdown) or environmental risks.

3.5.7 Other Risks: These are discussed below.

A. Strategic Risk: This risk results from a fundamental shift in the economy or political environment. Strategic risks usually affect the entire industry and are much more difficult to protect themselves. A few examples are: the fall of Berlin Wall, disintegration of Soviet Empire; Southeast Asian Banking Crisis in 1997, 2008 Sub-prime lending crisis, the recent European Economic Crisis; to name a few.

This is the risk arising out of certain strategic decisions taken by the banks for sustaining themselves in the present day scenario—for example, decision to open a subsidiary may run the risk of losses if the subsidiary does not do good business. Strategic risk is the risk of loss caused by a lack of a long-term development component in the bank's managing team. Strategic risk is the risk that arises from the inability to implement appropriate business plans and strategies, decisions with regard to allocation of resources or adaptability to dynamic changes in the business/operating environment. There are a number of other risk factors through which operations risk, credit risk and market risk may manifest. It should be recognised that many of these risk factors are interrelated, one results to other.

B. Reputation Risk: Reputation risk is the risk arising from negative public opinion. This risk may expose the institution to litigation, financial loss, or a decline in customer base.

C. Technology Risk: This risk is associated with computers and the communication technology which is being increasingly introduced in the banks. This entails the risk of obsolescence and the risk of losing business to better technologies.

D. Regulatory Risk: When owned funds alone are managed by an entity, it is natural that very few regulators operate and supervise them. However, as banks accept deposit from public, obviously better governance is expected of them. This entails multiplicity of regulatory controls. Many banks, having already gone for public issue, have a greater responsibility and accountability. As banks deal with public funds and money, they are subject to various regulations.

Many such regulators in India include the Reserve Bank of India (RBI), Securities and Exchange Board of India (SEBI), Department of Company Affairs (DCA), etc. Moreover, banks should ensure compliance of the applicable provisions of The Banking Regulation Act, The Companies Act, etc. Thus, all the banks run the risk of multiple regulations which inhibits free growth of business as focus on compliance of too many regulations leave little energy and time for developing new business. Banks should learn the art of playing their business activities within the regulatory controls.

E. Legal Risk: Legal risk is the risk of loss caused by penalties or sanctions originating from court disputes due to breach of contractual and legal obligations, and penalties and sanctions pronounced by a regulatory body. Legal risks are endemic in financial contracting and are separate from the legal ramifications of credit, counter party and operational risks. New statutes, tax legislations, court opinions and regulations can put formerly well-established transactions into contention even when all parties have previously performed adequately and are fully able to perform in the future. For example, environmental regulations have radically affected real estate values for older properties and imposed serious risks to lending institutions in this area.

A second type of legal risk arises from the activities of an institution's management or employees. Fraud, violations of regulations or laws, and other actions can lead to catastrophic loss, as recent examples in the thrift industry have demonstrated.

F. Environment Risk: With the passage of time, technological advancements take place, expectation of the customers change and enlarge. Customers are more quality conscious and want the best. Similarly, with the economic liberalization and globalization, more national and international players are operating the financial markets, particularly in the banking field. This provides the platform for environmental change and exposes the bank to environmental risks. Thus, unless the banks improve their delivery channels, reach customers, innovate their products that are service-oriented; they are exposed to the environment risk, resulting in loss in business share with consequential profit.

3.6 Role of RBI in Risk Management by Banks

The Reserve Bank of India has been using CAMELS rating to evaluate the financial soundness of the banks. The CAMELS Model consists of six components namely capital adequacy, asset quality, management, earnings quality, liquidity and sensitivity to market risk

In 1988, The Basel Committee on Banking Supervision of the Bank for International Settlements (BIS) had recommended using capital adequacy, assets quality, management quality and earnings and liquidity (CAMEL) as the criteria for assessing a financial institution (FI). The sixth component, sensitivity to market risk(s) was added to CAMEL in 1997 (Gilbert, Meyer and Vaughan, 2000). However, most of the developing countries are using CAMEL instead of CAMELS in the performance evaluation of the FIs. The central banks in some of the countries like Nepal and Kenya use CAEL instead of CAMELS (Baral, 2005). CAMELS' framework is a common method for evaluating the soundness of financial institutions.

In India, the focus of the statutory regulation of commercial banks by RBI until the early 1990s was mainly on licensing, administration of minimum capital requirements, pricing of services including administration of interest rates on deposits as well as credit, reserves and liquid asset requirements (Kannan, 2004). In these circumstances, the supervision had to focus essentially on solvency issues. After the evolution of the BIS prudential norms in 1988, the RBI took a series of measures to realign its supervisory and regulatory standards and bring it at par with international best practices. At the same time, it also took care to keep in view the socio-economic conditions of the country, the business practices, payment systems prevalent in the country and the predominantly agrarian nature of the economy, and ensured that the prudential norms were applied over the period and across different segments of the financial sector in a phased manner.

Finally, it was in the year 1999 that RBI recognised the need for an appropriate risk management and issued guidelines to banks regarding assets liability management, management of credit, market and operational risks. The entire supervisory mechanism has been realigned since 1994 under the directions of a newly constituted Board for Financial Supervision (BFS), which functions under the aegis of the RBI, to suit the demanding needs of a strong and stable financial system. The supervisory jurisdiction of the BFS now extends to the entire financial system barring the capital market institutions and the insurance sector. The periodical on-site inspections, and also the targeted appraisals by the Reserve Bank, are now supplemented by off-site surveillance which particularly focuses on the risk profile of the supervised institution. A process of rating of banks on the basis of CAMELS in respect of Indian banks and CACS (capital, asset quality, compliance and systems and control) in respect of foreign banks has been put in place from 1999.

Since then, the RBI has moved towards more stringent capital adequacy norms and adopted the CAMEL (capital adequacy, asset quality, management earnings, liquidity) based rating system for evaluating the soundness of Indian banks. The Reserve Bank's regulatory and supervisory responsibility has been widened to include financial institutions and non-banking financial companies. As a result, considering the changes in the banking industry, the thrust lies upon risk-based supervision (RBS). The main supervisory issues addressed by Board for Financial Supervision (BFS) relate to on-site and off-site supervision of banks.

The on-site supervision system for banks is on an annual cycle and is based on the 'CAMEL' model. It focuses on core assessments in accordance with the statutory mandate, i.e., solvency, liquidity, operational soundness and management prudence. Thus, banks are rated on this basis. Moreover, in view of the recent trends towards financial integration, competition, globalisation, it has become necessary for the BFS to supplement on-site supervision with off-site surveillance so as to capture 'early warning signals' from off-site monitoring that would be helpful to avert the likes of East Asian financial crisis (Sireesha, 2008). The off-site monitoring system consists of capital adequacy, asset quality, large credit and concentration, connected lending, earnings and risk exposures viz., currency, liquidity and interest rate risks. Apart from this, the fundamental and technical analysis of stock of banks in the secondary market will serve as a supplementary indicator of financial performance of banks.

Thus, on the basis of RBS, a risk profile of individual bank will be prepared. A high-risk sensitive bank will be subjected to more intensive supervision by shorter periodicity with greater use of supervisory tools, aimed at structural meetings, additional off site surveillance and regular on-site inspection etc. This will be undertaken in order to ensure the stability of the Indian financial system.

3.7 Risk Management by Bank: Basel Committee Approach

In order to help the banks to recognise the different kinds of risks and to take adequate steps to overcome the under-capitalisation of bank assets and lessen the credit and operational risks faced by banks, Bank for International Settlements (BIS) set up the Basel Committee on banking supervision in 1988, which issued guidelines for updating risk management in banks. These guidelines brought about standardization and universalization among the global banking committee for risk management and sought to protect the interest of the depositors/shareholders of the banks. As per the guidelines issued, capital adequacy was considered panacea for risk management and all banks were advised to have capital adequacy ratio (CAR) of at least 8 percent. CAR is the ratio of capital to risk weighted assets and it provides the cushion to the depositors in case of bankruptcy. In January 1999, the Basel Committee proposed a new capital accord, which is known as Basel II—a sound framework for measuring and quantifying the risk associated with banking operations put by it.

The emphasis of New Basel Accord was on flexibility, efficient operations and higher revenues for banks with full acknowledgement of risks. The New Accord made clear distinction between the credit risk, market risk and operational risk, stipulating assessment of risk weightage covering all the three categories separately. Also it provided a range of options for determining the capital requirements for credit risk and operational risk. Banks were required to select approaches that are most appropriate for their operations and financial markets. The finalised Basel II Accord was released in June 2004. The mid-term review of annual policy for the year 2006-07 from the Reserve Bank of India (RBI) revealed that the intended date for adoption of Basel II, i.e. March 2007, had to be postponed by two years, taking into consideration the stake of preparedness of the banking system in the country. This accord is based on three pillars, viz.:

- Pillar I: minimum capital requirement.
- Pillar II: supervisory review.
- Pillar III: market discipline.

3.7.1 Pillar I: Minimum Capital Requirement: The minimum capital requirement (MCR) is set by the capital ratio which is defined as (Total Capital - Tier I + Tier II + Tier III)/credit risk + market risk + operational risk). Basel I provided for only a credit risk charge. A market risk was implemented in 1996 amendments. In the initial stage, all banks were required to follow standardized approach in credit risk, basic indicator approach in operational risk and standardized duration approach in market risk. Migration to higher approaches would require RBI permission. Higher approaches are more risk sensitive and may reduce capital requirement for banks following sound risk management.

3.7.2 Pillar II: Supervisory Review Process: The supervisory review process is required to ensure adequacy as well as to ensure integrity by the risk management processes. The Basel Committee has stated four key principles of supervisory review as under:

- Bank should have a process for accessing its overall capital adequacy in relation to its risk profile, as well as, a strategy for maintaining its capital levels.
- Supervisors expect banks to operate above the minimum regulatory capital ratios and ensure banks hold capital in excess of the minimum.
- Supervisors shall review bank, internal capital adequacy assessment and strategy, as well as compliance with regulatory capital ratios.
- Supervisors shall seek to intervene at an early stage to prevent capital from falling below prudent levels.

The Reserve Bank of India being the supervisor of the banking operations in India is expected to evaluate how well banks are assessing their capital needs relative to their risks. When deficiencies are identified, prompt and decisive actions are expected to be taken by the supervisors to reduce the risk.

3.7.3 Pillar III: Market Discipline: Effective market discipline requires rateable and timely information that enables counter parties to make well established risk assessment. Pillar III relates to periodical disclosures to regulator, board of the bank and market, about various parameters which indicates the risk profile of the bank. Reserve Bank of India has stipulated that banks should provide all Pillar III disclosures, both quantitative and qualitative as at the end March each year along with the annual financial statement. The banks are required to put such disclosures on their websites. Market discipline promotes safety and soundness in banks and financial system and facilitates banks' conducting their business in a safe, sound and efficient manner.

3.8 Current Risk Status of Banks in India

Indian banks as a matter of fact do not suffer from situation/position of dangerous capital structure. The Basel III norms have stipulated minimum leverage ratio (percentage of minimum of Tier I capital to total assets ratio) of 4.5 percent. Based on the Basel III norms, following are indicators of the current leverage position of all scheduled commercial banks operating in India (Table 3.1).

Table 3.1: Leverage Position of Indian Banks

(₹ billion)

Head	2011-12	2012-13
Tier I Capital to Total Capital (*in percent*)	72.8	74.1
Total Capital and Reserves of all SCBs	6085.62	7089.30
Estimated Amount of Tier I Capital (All SCBs)	4430.33	5253.17
Total Assets Base of all SCBs	83,209	95,733
Leverage Ratio (Tier I Capital to Total Asset Ratio) (As per Basel III) (*in percent*)	5.30	5.48

Sources: (i) *Trends and Progress of Banking, 2013*; (ii) *Profile of Banks, 2012-13*, Reserve Bank of India.

3.9 Challenges in the Indian context

Basel II is intended to improve safety and soundness of the financial system by placing increased emphasis on bank's own internal control and risk management processes and models, the supervisory review process and market discipline. Indeed, to enable the calculation of capital requirements under the new accord, it requires a bank to implement a comprehensive risk management framework. However, these changes will also have wide ranging effects on bank's information technology systems, processes, people and business, beyond the regulatory compliance, risk management and finance functions.

Though every bank has to invest a lot of time, manpower

and energy in the implementations of Basel II, yet it helps the banks to assess the risks associated with the business effectively. More so, it facilitates the banks to produce quantified and more realistic measure of the risk. Basel II enables the banks to handle business with more confidence and make better business decisions. But the techniques and the methods suggested in the new accord would pose considerable implementation challenges for the banks, especially in a developing country like India. Some of them are described as under:

- Implementation of the new framework will require substantial resources and commitment on the part of both banks and supervisors. Banks are required to make enormous improvements in the areas of policies, organisational structure, MIS, tools for analysis, process, specified training of staff etc. It will involve huge cost both for the banks as well as for the supervisors.
- The new norms will increase the capital requirements in all the banks due to introduction of multiple risk weights with preferential treatment for high rated assets. However, the capital requirement for credit risk may go down due to adoption of more risk sensitive techniques such as securitization, derivatives, melting services, equity holdings, venture capital and guarantees etc.
- Risk management is extremely data-intensive. Accurate, reliable and timely availability of data is crucial for proper risk management. Banks need to implement substantial changes to their internal systems to prepare for appropriate data collection and revised reporting requirements. These changes may require systems integration, modification and introduction of new software. Banks need to assess the capabilities of their present systems and review the necessary system changes required.
- To provide the basis for forecasting and building of models in respect of various activities, such as loaning, security and foreign exchange transactions, a lot of

historical data is required. In the Indian context, major handicap is the absence of data series, particularly related to the transactions in individual loan accounts.

The new capital accord assigns risk-weight of sovereign between 0-50 percent. There is also a higher risk weight accorded to small and medium enterprises. In India, the PSBs have more than 40 percent of their lending to priority sector. The implementation of Basel II can adversely affect the priority sector lending. Some issues are detailed below:

- Even the G-10 countries are finding it difficult to implement the Basel II accord in all the banks. Therefore, longer time may be required for its implementation in some or all the banks in India.
- In India, credit rating is restricted to issues and not to the issuers. While Basel II gives some scope to extend the rating of issues to issuers, this would be an approximation and it would be necessary for the system to move to the rating of issuers. Encouraging rating of issuers would be a challenge.
- Yet another requirement for establishing risk management system is trained and skilled manpower. The managers should understand both the theory and practice of risk. To reach such on understanding undoubtedly involves a continuous learning process in the new technologies. Inducting a continuous learning process in the line managers and educating them in risk management is a task to be addressed on priority by the banks for the smooth adoption of the risk management principles and practices and Basel II recommendations across the banks. Skill development for risk management approaches, both at the bank level and at supervisors' level, would be a tough task ahead.

3.10 Risk Management Scenario in the Future

Risk management activities will be more pronounced in future banking because of liberalization, deregulation and global integration of financial markets. This would be adding

2.11.6 Tone at the Top: Effective risk management programme starts with 'The Tone at the Top'—driven by the top management and adhered by the bottom line. However, if bank's top leaders perceive operational risk management solely as a regulatory mandate, rather than as an important means of enhancing competitiveness and performance, they may tend to be less supportive of such efforts. Management and the board must understand the importance of operational risk, demonstrate their support for its management, and designate an appropriate managing entity and framework—one that is a part of the bank's overall corporate governance framework.

By adopting an integrated operational risk framework, companies can ensure that all operational risk management initiatives are sustained and are aligned with the corporate strategy.

3

Risk Management in Banking Business

3.1 History of Indian Banking

The banking industry in India has a huge canvas of history, which covers the traditional banking practices from the time of British Government to the reforms period, nationalization to privatization of banks and now increasing numbers of foreign banks in India. Therefore, banking in India has been through a long journey. Banking industry in India has also achieved a new height with the changing times. The use of technology has brought a revolution in the working style of the banks. Nevertheless, the fundamental aspects of banking i.e. trust and the confidence of the people on the institution remain the same. The majority of the banks are still successful in keeping with the confidence of the shareholders as well as other stakeholders. However, the changing dynamics of banking business has brought new kinds of risk exposure.

The financial sector in various economies—like that of India—is undergoing a monumental change, factoring into account world events such as the 'banking crisis' across the globe a few years back. The various aspects of increasing global competition to Indian banks by foreign banks, increased deregulation, introduction of innovative products and financial instruments as well as innovation in delivery channels, have highlighted the need for Indian banks to be prepared in terms of risk management. Indian banks have been making great advancements in terms of technology, quality, as well as stability such that they have started to expand and diversify at a rapid rate.

However, such expansion brings these banks into the context of risk, especially with the onset of increased globalization and liberalization. In banks and other financial

4

Interest Rate Risks

Interest rate risk is an integral part of banking business, and may even be a source of profit. Interest rate risk is a term which is totally unknown in India and has suddenly become relevant with certain changes in the banking industry. Till 1970, the regulatory restrictions on banks greatly reduced many of the risks in the financial system. The phrase '3-6-3' i.e., banks bring in short-term deposits at 3 percent, lend at 6 percent and be home for the day by 3 p.m. became a common reference about the bankers. In 1950s and 1960s, banks considered only the credit and liquidity risks as major constraints on profitability. Deregulation of the banking system in the 1970s, however got many bankers unprepared to manage interest rate risk to which their institutions were suddenly exposed. Many bank failures in the world during 1970s, 1980s, and 1990s were triggered out of poorly managed interest rate risks. Many financial institutions funded their long-term fixed assets with short-term volatile liabilities. The earning of assets and the cost of liabilities are closely related to interest rate volatility. However, today insulating interest spread against frequent interest rate changes has become the major strategic objective of a bank's management.

4.1 Interest Rate Defined

An interest rate is the cost of borrowing money or the return for investing money. It is the rate at which interest is paid by a borrower (debtor) for the use of money that they borrow from a lender (creditor). Specifically, the interest rate is a percentage of principal paid a certain number of times (m) per period (usually quoted per year). For example, a small company borrows capital from a bank to buy new assets for its business, and in return the lender receives interest at a predetermined interest rate for deferring the use of funds and instead lending it to the borrower.

In the past two centuries, interest rates have been variously set either by national governments or central banks. For example, the Federal Reserve's federal funds rate in the United States varied between 0.25 percent to 19 percent from 1954 to 2008, while the Bank of England's base rate varied between 0.5 percent and 15 percent from 1989 to 2009. Interest rates are normally expressed as a percentage of the principal for a period of one year. Interest rate targets are a vital tool of monetary policy and are taken into account when dealing with variables like investment, inflation and unemployment. The central banks of countries generally tend to reduce interest rates when they wish to increase investment and consumption in a country's economy. However, a low interest rate as a macro-economic policy can be risky and may lead to the creation of an economic bubble in which large amounts of investments are poured into the real estate market and stock market. In developed economies, interest rate adjustments are thus made to keep inflation within a target range for the health of the economy.

Interest rate risk is a normal part of banking and can be an important source of profitability and shareholder value. Excessive interest rate risk can pose a significant threat to a bank's earnings and capital base. Changes in interest rates affect bank's earnings by changing its net interest income and the level of other interest sensitive income and operating expenses. Changes in interest rates also affect the underlying value of the bank's assets, liabilities and off-balance sheet (OBS) instruments because the present value of future cash flows change when interest rate changes. Market value of an asset or liability is equal to the present value of current and future cash flows from the assets and liabilities. Therefore, rising interest rates increase the discount rate on those cash flows and decrease the market value of the asset or liability.

behalf of the customer. In most cases, the broker asks for a fee in exchange of its services. This fee can be a fixed or percentage-based commission, or a combination of both.

3.2.2 Asset Transformation Function: The asset transformation function translates the product specifications requested by the savers to products requested by the borrowers. Savers, e.g. retail deposit savers, are more attracted by products with lower price risk, liquidity costs and monitoring costs. Borrowers, e.g., large corporations are more interested in long-term debt but carry a higher risk, i.e. the uncertainty about their pay back of the debt. Banks transform the safe, short-term and liquid small amounts of savings deposits to risky long-term debt to firms or firm borrowers. Banks have a sufficient number of risk experts to analyse the risk profile of the borrowers.

In their role as a financial intermediary, banks reduce market deficiencies on three domains.

3.2.3 Liquidity Intermediation: The bank matches the objectives of two main groups in the economy viz. consumers and investors. Consumers and household savers have a short-term horizon on which they want to optimize their utility function. Consumers prefer a smooth consumption pattern to minimize changes in utility and hold liquid reserves to absorb temporary shocks in purchasing power, e.g. due to unemployment or unexpected expenses (e.g. a broken car). Investors need long-term financing for long-term projects and may have short-term cash difficulties. This financing bears a higher risk. Such loans or debt is illiquid for whosoever provides it. Banks provide savings account deposits that provide a liquidity insurance for the consumers. The cost of the liquidity premium is covered by reduced interest rate. At the same time, banks use the savings deposits to provide for long-term illiquid investments. This is possible when the amount of deposits a bank holds is sufficiently stable over time by the law of large numbers.

3.2.4 Risk Intermediation: Banks provide low-risk saving deposit products to consumer and invest their deposits in more risky debt and other assets. This is possible by a good risk management and sufficient diversification. Banks hold sufficiently diversified portfolios in which the risk of an individual loan is reduced.

Not all loans will default at the same time. In general, banks transform different types of risk (credit, market, exchange rate, interest rate risk) and repackage it into an appropriate product for all economic agents. Another example is the securitization activity, where a risky portfolio is structured into various products with specific risk profiles tailored to the needs of different economic agents.

3.2.5 Information Intermediation: Information gathering is important to avoid economic pitfalls due to asymmetric information. Firm entrepreneurs are typically much better informed than the consumer savers. Such information asymmetry may have adverse impacts on the economy, known as the moral hazard and adverse selection problem.

In reality, we can say that management of financial institution is nothing but a management of risk. Managing financial risk systematically and professionally becomes an even more important task. Rising global competition, increasing deregulation, introduction of innovative products and delivery channels have pushed risk management to the forefront of today's financial landscape. Ability to gauge the risks and take appropriate position will be the key to success. It can be said that risk takers will survive, effective risk managers will prosper and risk averse are likely to perish. The risk arises due to uncertainties, which in turn arise due to changes taking place in prevailing economic, social and political environment and lack of non-availability of information concerning such changes. Risk is an exposure to a transaction with loss, which occurs with some probability and which can be expected, measured and minimized. In financial institutions, risk results from variations and fluctuations in assets or liability or both in income from assets or payments and on liabilities or in outflows and inflows of cash. Today, structure of the mismatch position. If interest rate rises, the cost of funds increases more rapidly than the yield on assets, thereby reducing the net income.

Interest rate risk is broadly classified into mismatch or gap risk, basis risk, net interest position risk, embedded option risk, yield curve risk, price risk and reinvestment risk. Typically, interest rate risk is split into: (i) traded interest rate risk; and (ii) non-traded interest rate risk (balance sheet). Interest rate risk in the banking book arises from a bank's core banking activities. Interest rate risk management has become very important and assorted instruments have been developed to deal with interest rate risk.

Thus, an effective risk management process that maintains interest rate risk within prudential levels is essential to the safety and soundness of banks. Various banks have already identified interest rate risk, its impact on profitability and have started assessing the magnitude of interest rate risk embedded in their balance sheets.

Interest rate risk is the risk to income or capital arising from fluctuating interest rates. Changes in interest rates affect a banking corporation's earnings by changing its net interest income and the level of other income (including changes in non-interest revenues/expenses). Changes in interest rates also affect the underlying value of the banking corporation's assets, liabilities and off-balance sheet (OBS) financial instruments because the present value of future cash flows (and in some cases, the cash flows themselves) change when interest rates change. Banking corporations encounter interest rate risk in several ways, including repricing risk, yield curve risk, basis risk (also known as spread risk), and other risks.

4.4 Various Types of Interest Risks

4.4.1 Repricing or Maturity Mismatch Risk: A gap or mismatch risk arises from holding assets and liabilities with different principal amounts, maturity dates or repricing dates, thereby creating exposure to changes in the level of interest rates. The gap is the difference between the amount of assets and liabilities on which the interest rates are reset during a given period. As financial intermediaries, banks encounter interest rate risk in several ways. The primary and most often discussed form of interest rate risk arises from timing differences in the maturity (for fixed rate) and repricing (for floating rate) of bank assets, liabilities and off-balance sheet (OBS) positions.

While such repricing mismatches are fundamental to the business of banking, they can expose a bank's income and underlying economic value to unanticipated fluctuations as interest rates vary. For instance, a bank that funded a long-term fixed rate loan with a short-term deposit could face a decline in both the future income arising from the position and its underlying value if interest rates increase. These declines arise because the cash flows on the loan are fixed over its lifetime, while the interest paid on the funding is variable, and increases after the short-term deposit matures.

4.4.2 Yield Curve Risk: A yield curve is a line on a graph plotting the yield of all maturities of a particular instrument. Yield curve changes its slope and shape from time to time depending upon repricing and various other factors. Yield curve risk arises when unanticipated shifts of the yield curve have adverse effects on a bank's income or underlying economic value. For instance, the underlying economic value of a long position in 10-year government bonds hedged by a short position in 5-year government notes could decline sharply if the yield curve steepens, even if the position is hedged against parallel movements in the yield curve. As the economy moves through business cycle, the yield curve changes rather frequently. The yield curve can be twisted to the desired direction by altering the yields on government stocks or different maturities. Thus, banks should evaluate the movement in yield curves and the impact of that on the portfolio values and income.

have provided a platform to the banks for creating an environment for efficient customer services as also for designing new products. In fact, it is the technological innovation that has helped banks to manage the assets and liabilities in a better way, providing various delivery channels, reducing processing time of transactions and reducing manual intervention in back office functions etc. However, all these developments have also increased the diversity and complexity of risks, which need to be managed professionally so that the opportunities provided by the technology are not negated.

3.4 What Kinds of Risks Are Being Absorbed?

The risks contained in the bank's principle activities, i.e., those involving its own balance sheet and its basic business of lending and borrowing, are not all borne by the bank itself. In many instances, the institution will eliminate or mitigate the financial risk associated with a transaction by proper business practices; in others, it will shift the risk to other parties through a combination of pricing and product design.

The banking industry recognizes that an institution need not engage in business in a manner that unnecessarily imposes risk upon it; nor should it absorb risk that can be efficiently transferred to other participants. Rather, it should only manage risks at the firm level that are more efficiently managed there than by the market itself or by their owners in their own portfolios. In short, it should accept only those risks that are uniquely a part of the bank's array of services.

Elsewhere, Oldfield and Santomero (1997) argued that risks facing all financial institutions can be segmented into three separable types, from a management perspective. These are as under:

- Risks that can be eliminated or avoided by simple business practices.
- Risks that can be transferred to other participants.
- Risks that must be actively managed at the firm level.

In the first of these cases, the practice of risk avoidance involves actions to reduce the chances of idiosyncratic losses from standard banking activity by eliminating risks that are superfluous to the institution's business purpose. Common risk avoidance practices here include at least three types of actions. The standardization of process, contracts and procedures to prevent inefficient or incorrect financial decisions is the first of these. The construction of portfolios that benefit from diversification across borrowers and that reduce the effects of any one loss experience is another. Finally, the implementation of incentive-compatible contracts with the institution's management to require that employees be held accountable is the third. In each case the goal is to rid the firm of risks that are not essential to the financial service provided, or to absorb only an optimal quantity of a particular kind of risk.

There are also some risks that can be eliminated, or at least substantially reduced through the technique of risk transfer. Markets exist for many of the risks borne by the banking firm. Interest rate risk can be transferred by interest rate products such as swaps or other derivatives. Borrowing terms can be altered to effect a change in their duration. Finally, the bank can buy or sell financial claims to diversify or concentrate the risks that result in from servicing its client base. To the extent that the financial risks of the assets created by the firm are understood by the market, these assets can be sold at their fair value. Unless the institution has a comparative advantage in managing the attendant risk and/or a desire for the embedded risk they contain, there is no reason for the bank to absorb such risks, rather than transfer them.

However, there are two classes of assets or activities where the risk inherent in the activity must and should be absorbed at the bank level. In these cases, good reasons exist for using firm resources to manage bank level risk. The first of these includes financial assets or activities where the nature of the embedded risk may be complex and difficult to communicate to third parties. This is the case when the bank institutions are typically subject to option risk in the form of embedded options in retail products. These options occur on both the asset and the liability side of the balance sheet. On the asset side of the balance sheet, prepayment options are the most common form of embedded option. Mortgage and consumer loans can give the customer (particularly in the United States) the option of prepayment free of penalty, or subject to a very small penalty. A prepayment option is equivalent to the writing of a call option to the customer.

This means that in an environment of falling interest rates, customers will prepay their mortgages and/or consumer loans, as a result of which the duration of the assets of the banking book may be reduced. The increased cash inflows generated by the prepayments will be reinvested by the institution at lower interest rates. This acceleration of prepayments is also referred to as the reinvestment or prepayment risk. In an environment of rising interest rates, the opposite occurs as prepayments are delayed, resulting in potential increase in the duration of the assets. This delay in prepayments is also referred to as extension risk.

On the liability side of the balance sheet, the most common form of option is the customer's right to make early withdrawals from sight deposits and savings deposits (non-maturity deposits). The early withdrawal right is equivalent to a put option: if interest rates rise, the market value of deposits decline and customers have the right to exercise the put by withdrawing the deposits, and to reinvest the proceeds in higher yielding products. This option works in the favour of the deposit holder. The institution's discretion of pricing retail products as non-maturity deposits can also be seen as a type of option. This type of option favours the institution: if market interest rates are rising, an institution's pricing response can lag behind the change in the market, whereas in the case of falling market interest rates, the institution's pricing response can lead the market. The techniques used by institutions to analyse the forms of option risk vary from traditional gap analysis to income simulation and economic value models.

4.5 Effects of Interest Rate Risk

Interest rate risk can be viewed from the perspective of earnings (or accrual accounting) and/or economic value. In the case of the earnings perspective, the focus is on the impact of interest rate movements on the net interest or accrued income of a bank over a time horizon of one to two years. This is the traditional approach used by banks to assess their interest rate risk position. As a result of the relatively short time horizon of one to two years, the potential impact of interest rate movements on long-term positions is not analysed adequately. For this reason, particularly in the case of larger institutions, interest rate risk management policy also takes account of the economic value perspective as well as the earnings perspective.

The economic value perspective focuses on the potential impact of interest rate movements on the market values of an institution's assets, liabilities and off-balance sheet instruments. Using the economic value perspective, the potential impact of interest rate movements on the present value of all future cash flows is analysed based upon the current composition of the balance sheet. It, therefore, supplements the information provided by the earnings perspective of interest rate risk by analysing the potential long-term effects of interest rate movements.

Management of interest rate risk aims at capturing the risks arising from the maturity and repricing mismatches and is measured both from the earnings and economic value perspective. Interest rate changes can have adverse effects both on a bank's earnings and its economic value. This has given rise to two separate, but complementary, perspectives for assessing a bank's interest rate risk exposure.

4.6 Measurement of Interest Rate Risk

A variety of techniques and models are used by

The main differences between the two are: (a) assets that are held for trading are put in the trading book, assets that are held to maturity are held in the banking book; (b) assets in the trading book are marked-to-market daily and assets in the banking book are held at historic cost; (c) the value-at-risk for assets in the trading book is calculated at a 99 percent confidence level based on a 10-day time horizon. The value-at-risk for assets in the banking books are calculated at a 99.9 percent confidence level on a one-year horizon.

3.4.3 Off-balance Sheet Exposures: Off-balance sheet exposures are contingent in nature. These contingencies adversely affect the revenue generation of banks. Banks may also have contingency receivables.

Here, banks are the beneficiaries, subject to certain contingencies. Derivatives are off-balance sheet market exposures. They may be swaps, futures, forward contracts, foreign currency contracts, options etc. Contingent exposure may become a fund-based exposure.

Such exposures may become a part of the banking book or trading book, depending on the nature of the off-balance sheet exposure. Therefore, off-balance sheet exposures may include liquidity risk, interest rate risk, default or credit risk and operational risk.

3.5 Types of Risks Banks Face

Banks that manage their risks have a competitive advantage. They take risks consciously, anticipate adverse changes and protect themselves from such changes. In view of growing complexity of banks' business and the dynamic operating environment, risk management has become very significant, especially in the financial sector. As stated earlier, the term *risk* and the types associated to it would refer to mean financial risk or uncertainty of financial loss. If we consider risk in terms of probability of occurrence frequently, we measure risk on a scale, with certainty of occurrence at one end and certainty of non-occurrence at the other end. Risk is the greatest where the probability of occurrence or non-occurrence is equal.

Risk at the apex level may be visualized as the probability of a bank's financial health being impaired due to one or more contingent factors. While the parameters indicating the banks' health may vary from net interest margin to market value of equity, the factor which can cause hurt the most are also numerous.

For instance, there could be default in repayment of loans by borrowers or change in value of assets or disruption of operation due to reason like technological failure. These factors may be classified as credit risk and market risk.

The Reserve Bank of India guidelines issued in October 1999 has identified and categorized the majority of risk into three major categories assumed to be encountered by banks and these are credit risk, market risk and operational risk.

The types of risks can be fundamentally sub-divided in two categories, i.e. financial and non-financial risk. Financial risks would involve all those aspects which deal mainly with financial aspects of the bank. These can be further sub-divided into credit risk and market risk. Both credit and market risk may be further sub-divided.

Non-financial risks would entail all the risks faced by the banks in their regular workings, i.e. operational risk, strategic risk, funding risk, political risk and legal risk.

Non-financial risk refers to those risks that may affect a bank's business growth, marketability of its product and services, likely failure of its strategies aimed at business growth etc. These risks may arise on account of management failures, competition, non-availability of suitable products/services, external factors etc.

Thus, the risks to which a bank is particularly exposed in its operations are: liquidity risk, credit risk, market risks (interest rate risk, foreign exchange risk and risk from change in market price of securities, financial derivatives and commodities), exposure risks, investment risks, risks relating and OBS positions into a certain number of predefined time bands according to their maturity (if fixed rate) or time remaining for their next repricing (if floating rate). The risk sensitive assets and risk sensitive liabilities are grouped into maturity buckets based on maturity and the time until the first possible repricing due to change in the interest rates.

Simple maturity/repricing schedules can be used to generate simple indicators of the interest rate risk sensitivity of both earnings and economic value to changing interest rates. When this approach is used to assess the interest rate risk of current earnings, it is typically referred to as gap analysis. Gap analysis was one of the first methods developed to measure a bank's interest rate risk exposure, and continues to be widely used by banks. The objective of this analysis is to improve net interest income in the short-run over discreet periods of time called the gap periods. To evaluate earnings exposure, interest rate sensitive liabilities in each time band are subtracted from the corresponding interest rate sensitive assets to produce a repricing 'gap' for that time band.

This gap can be multiplied by an assumed change in interest rates to yield an approximation of the change in net interest income that would result from such an interest rate movement.

The size of the interest rate movement used in the analysis can be based on a variety of factors, including historical experience, simulation of potential future interest rate movements, and the judgement of bank management. A negative, or liability-sensitive, gap occurs when liabilities exceed assets (including off-balance sheet positions) in a given time band. This means that an increase in market interest rates could cause a decline in net interest income. Conversely, a positive, or asset-sensitive, gap implies that the bank's net interest income could decline as a result of a decrease in the level of interest rates.

A number of time bands can be used while constructing a gap report. Generally, most of the banks focus their attention on near-term periods, viz. monthly, quarterly, half-yearly or one year. It is very difficult to take a view on interest rate movements beyond a year. Banks with large exposures in the short-term should test the sensitivity of their assets and liabilities even at shorter intervals like overnight, 1-7 days, 8-14 days, etc.

Although gap analysis is a very commonly used approach for assessing interest rate risk exposure, it has a number of shortcomings. First, gap analysis does not take account of variation in the characteristics of different positions within a time band. In particular, all positions within a given time band are assumed to mature or reprice simultaneously, a simplification that is likely to have greater impact on the precision of the estimates as the degree of aggregation within a time band increases.

Moreover, gap analysis ignores differences in spreads between interest rates that could arise as the level of market interest rates changes (basis risk). In addition, it does not take into account any changes in the timing of payments that might occur as a result of changes in the interest rate environment. Thus, it fails to account for differences in the sensitivity of income that may arise from option-related positions. For these reasons, gap analysis provides only a rough approximation to the actual change in net interest income which would result from the chosen change in the pattern of interest rates. Finally, most gap analysis fail to capture variability in non-interest revenue and expenses, a potentially important source of risk to current income.

4.6.3 Value at Risk (VaR): The VaR method is an economic value method that measures the potential loss of market value from the positioning on one or more yield curves resulting from interest rate movements. When calculating the VaR, statistical techniques such as frequency distributions, standard deviations and variance-covariance matrices can be used to analyse the risk of a portfolio and the relationships existing in the portfolio. Strictly speaking, VaR measures the expected maximum loss in terms of interest rate risk that can be incurred under normal market circumstances on a fixed-income security or portfolio over a given time horizon and subject to a given confidence level. When the VaR method is applied to the banking book, a time horizon should be considered that is in accordance with the policy intention of holding positions for a longer period of time.

This is in contrast to the one-day VaR that is applicable to trading books, where the policy intention is to trade positions daily. If the VaR is measured over a longer time horizon, such as the banking book (e.g. over a time horizon of one year), the potential loss needs to be seen in relation to the expected return. The expected economic return needs to be measured over a time horizon corresponding to that used for the VaR calculation. This is also referred to as the relative VaR, being the difference between the absolute VaR and the expected return.

The VaR approach covers three different techniques, which are the analytical variance-covariance method, the full valuation historical simulation and the Monte Carlo simulation techniques. Each of these techniques is associated with disadvantages or shortcomings. For example, the variance-covariance method assumes that the returns are normally distributed statistically and that the portfolios are a linear combination of the underlying positions, which makes this method less appropriate for portfolios with high optionality. The historical simulation method is purely backward looking and requires a large volume of data, or a long observation period, in order to ensure the reliability of the results, whereas the Monte Carlo simulation method is very demanding in terms of system technology.

4.7 BCBS Principles for Interest Rate Risk Management

The Basel Committee on Banking Supervision (BCBS) issued a paper on principles for the management of interest rate risk in September 1997. In developing these principles, the Committee drew on supervisory guidance in member countries, on the comments of the banking industry on the Committee's earlier paper, issued for consultation in April 1993, and on comments received on the draft paper issued for consultation. In addition, the paper incorporated many of the principles contained in the guidance issued by the Committee for derivative activities, which are reflected in the qualitative parameters for model-users in the capital standards for market risk. This revised version of the 1997 paper is being issued to support the Pillar 2 approach to interest rate risk in the banking book in The New Basel Capital Accord. The revision is reflected especially in this Summary, in Principles 12 to 15. Principles 1 to 11 are general and intended for management of both trading book and banking book interest rate risk. Principles 12 to 15 specifically refer to interest rate risk in the banking book.

4.7.1 Board and Senior Management Oversight of Interest Rate Risk:

Principle 1: In order to carry out its responsibilities, the board of directors in a bank should approve strategies and policies with respect to interest rate risk management and ensure that senior management takes the steps necessary to monitor and control these risks. The board of directors should be informed regularly of the interest rate risk exposure of the bank in order to assess the monitoring and controlling of such risk.

Principle 2: Senior management must ensure that the structure of the bank's business and the level of interest rate risk it assumes are effectively managed, that appropriate policies and procedures are established to control and limit these risks, and that resources are available for evaluating and controlling interest rate risk.

Principle 3: Banks should clearly define the individuals and/or committees responsible for managing interest rate risk and should ensure that there is adequate separation of duties in key elements of the risk management process to avoid potential conflicts of interest. Banks should have risk measurement, monitoring and control functions with clearly defined duties that are sufficiently independent from position-taking functions of the bank and which report risk exposures directly to senior management and the board of directors. Larger or more complex banks should have a designated independent unit responsible for the design and administration of the bank's interest rate risk measurement, monitoring and control functions.

4.7.2 Adequate Risk Management Policies and Procedures:

Principle 4: It is essential that banks' interest rate risk policies and procedures are clearly defined and consistent with the nature and complexity of their activities. These policies should be applied on a consolidated basis and, as appropriate, at the level of individual affiliates, especially when recognising legal distinctions and possible obstacles to cash movements among affiliates.

Principle 5: It is important that banks identify the risks inherent in new products and activities and ensure these are subject to adequate procedures and controls before being introduced or undertaken. Major hedging or risk management initiatives should be approved in advance by the board or its appropriate delegated committee.

4.7.3 Risk Measurement, Monitoring and Control Functions:

Principle 6: It is essential that banks have interest rate risk measurement systems that capture all material sources of interest rate risk and that assess the effect of interest rate changes in ways that are consistent with the scope of their activities. The assumptions underlying the system should be clearly understood by risk managers and bank management.

Principle 7: Banks must establish and enforce operating limits and other practices that maintain exposures within levels consistent with their internal policies.

Principle 8: Banks should measure their vulnerability to loss under stressful market conditions—including the breakdown of key assumptions—and consider those results when establishing and reviewing their policies and limits for interest rate risk.

Principle 9: Banks must have adequate information systems for measuring, monitoring, controlling and reporting interest rate exposures. Reports must be provided on a timely basis to the bank's board of directors, senior management and, where appropriate, to individual business line managers.

4.7.4 Internal Controls:

Principle 10: Banks must have an adequate system of internal controls over their interest rate risk management process. A fundamental component of the internal control system involves regular independent reviews and evaluations of the effectiveness of the system and, where necessary, ensuring that appropriate revisions or enhancements to internal controls are made. The results of such reviews should be available to the relevant supervisory authorities.

4.7.5 Information for Supervisory Authorities:

Principle 11: Supervisory authorities should obtain from banks, sufficient and timely information with which to evaluate their level of interest rate risk. This information should take appropriate account of the range of maturities and currencies in each bank's portfolio, including off-balance sheet items, as well as other relevant factors, such as the distinction between trading and non-trading activities.

4.7.6 Capital Adequacy:

Principle 12: Banks must hold capital commensurate with the level of interest rate risk they undertake.

4.7.7 Disclosure of Interest Rate Risk:

Principle 13: Banks should release to the public, information on the level of interest rate risk and their policies for its management.

4.7.8 Supervisory Treatment of Interest Rate Risk in the Banking Book:

Principle 14: Supervisory authorities must assess whether the internal measurement systems of banks adequately capture the interest rate risk in their banking book. If a bank's internal measurement system does not adequately capture the interest rate risk, banks must bring the system to the required standard. To facilitate supervisors' monitoring of interest rate risk exposures across institutions, banks must provide the results of their internal measurement systems, expressed in terms of the threat to economic value, using a standardised interest rate shock.

Principle 15: If supervisors determine that a bank is not holding capital commensurate with the level of interest rate risk in the banking book, they should consider remedial action, requiring the bank either to reduce its risk, to hold a specific additional amount of capital, or a combination of both.

4.8 Sound Interest Rate Risk Management Practices

Sound interest rate risk management involves the application of four basic elements in the management of assets, liabilities and off-balance sheet instruments:

- Appropriate board and senior management oversight.
- Adequate risk management policies and procedures.
- Appropriate risk measurement, monitoring and control functions.
- Comprehensive internal controls and independent audits.

Effective oversight by a bank's board of directors and senior management is critical to a sound interest rate risk management process. It is essential that these individuals are aware of their responsibilities with regard to interest rate risk management and that they adequately perform their roles in overseeing and managing interest rate risk. The board of directors has the ultimate responsibility for understanding the nature and the level of interest rate risk taken by the bank. The board should approve broad business strategies and policies that govern or influence the interest rate risk of the bank. It should review the overall objectives of the bank with respect to interest rate risk and should ensure the provision of clear guidance regarding the level of interest rate risk acceptable to the bank. The board should also approve policies that identify lines of authority and responsibility for managing interest rate risk exposures.

Accordingly, the board of directors is responsible for approving the overall policies of the bank with respect to interest rate risk and for ensuring that management takes the steps necessary to identify, measure, monitor, and control these risks. The board or a specific committee of the board should periodically review information that is sufficient in detail and timeliness to allow it to understand and assess the performance of senior management in monitoring and controlling these risks in compliance with the bank's board-approved policies.

Such reviews should be conducted regularly, being carried out more frequently where the bank holds significant positions in complex instruments. In addition, the board or one of its committees should periodically re-evaluate significant interest rate risk management policies as well as overall business strategies that affect the interest rate risk exposure of the bank. The board of directors should encourage discussions between its members and senior management—as well as between senior management and others in the bank—regarding the bank's interest rate risk exposures and management process. Board members need not have detailed technical knowledge of complex financial instruments, legal issues, or of sophisticated risk management techniques. They have the responsibility, however, to ensure that senior management has a full understanding of the risks incurred by the bank and that the bank has personnel available who have the necessary technical skills to evaluate and control these risks. Management is also responsible for maintaining:

- Appropriate limits on risk taking.
- Adequate systems and standards for measuring risk.
- Standards for valuing positions and measuring performance.
- A comprehensive interest rate risk reporting and interest

rate risk management review process.

- Effective internal controls.

The specific manner in which a bank applies these elements in managing its interest rate risk will depend upon the complexity and nature of its holdings and activities as well as on the level of interest rate risk exposure. What constitutes adequate interest rate risk management practices can therefore vary considerably. For example, less complex banks whose senior managers are actively involved in the details of day-to-day operations may be able to rely on relatively basic interest rate risk management processes. However, other organisations that have more complex and wide-ranging activities are likely to require more elaborate and formal interest rate risk management processes, to address their broad range of financial activities and to provide senior management with the information they need to monitor and direct day-to-day activities.

Moreover, the more complex interest rate risk management processes employed at such banks require adequate internal controls that include audits or other appropriate oversight mechanisms to ensure the integrity of the information used by senior officials in overseeing compliance with policies and limits. The duties of the individuals involved in the risk measurement, monitoring and control functions must be sufficiently separate and independent from the business decision makers and position takers to ensure the avoidance of conflicts of interest. The Committee believes that interest rate risk should be monitored on a consolidated, comprehensive basis, to include interest rate exposures in subsidiaries.

At the same time, however, institutions should fully recognise any legal distinctions and possible obstacles to cash flow movements among affiliates and adjust their risk management process accordingly. While consolidation may provide a comprehensive measure in respect of interest rate risk, it may also underestimate risk when positions in one affiliate are used to offset positions in another affiliate. This is because a conventional accounting consolidation may allow theoretical offsets between such positions from which a bank may not in practice be able to benefit because of legal or operational constraints. Management should recognise the potential for consolidated measures to understate risks in such circumstances.

Interest rate risk reports to senior management should provide aggregate information as well as sufficient supporting detail to enable management to assess the sensitivity of the institution to changes in market conditions and other important risk factors. Senior management should also review periodically the organisation's interest rate risk management policies and procedures to ensure that they remain appropriate and sound. Senior management should also encourage and participate in discussions with members of the board and, where appropriate to the size and complexity of the bank, with risk management staff regarding risk measurement, reporting and management procedures.

Banks should clearly identify the individuals and/or committees responsible for conducting all of the various elements of interest rate risk management. Senior management should define lines of authority and responsibility for developing strategies, implementing tactics and conducting the risk measurement and reporting functions of the interest rate risk management process. Senior management should also provide reasonable assurance that all activities and all aspects of interest rate risk are covered by a bank's risk management process.

5

Credit Risks and Credit Derivatives

5.1 Credit Risk Defined

The field of credit risk gained considerable momentum due to the increased competition in the field and the challenges of the present financial crisis. Credit risk is one of the main risks of commercial banks that will affect the banks' ability of sustainable operations. Banks assume credit risk when they act as intermediaries of funds and credit risk management lies at the heart of commercial banking. Studies of banking crises show that the most frequent factor in the failure of banks has been poor loan quality. The credit risk management process of a bank is believed to be a good indicator of the quality of the bank's loan portfolio. Credit risk emerged as a significant risk management issue during the 1990s. In increasingly competitive markets, banks began taking on greater credit risk in this period. In a 1996 report, the Bank for International Settlements (BIS), defined credit risk as the risk that a counterparty will not settle an obligation for full value, either when due or at any time thereafter. In exchange for value systems, the risk is generally defined to include replacement risk and principal risk.

Credit risk is the bank's risk of loss arising from a borrower who does not make payments as promised. Such an event is termed as default. Credit risk involves inability or unwillingness of a customer or counterparty to meet commitments in relation to lending, trading, hedging, settlement and other financial transactions. Another term for credit risk is default risk. The risk of loss of principal or loss of a financial reward stemming from a borrower's failure to repay a loan or otherwise to meet a contractual obligation is termed as credit risk.

Credit risk arises whenever a borrower is expecting to use

future cash flows to pay a current debt. Banks are compensated for assuming credit risk by way of interest payments from the borrower or issuer of a debt obligation. The credit risk is generally made up of transaction risk or default risk and portfolio risk. The portfolio risk in turn comprises intrinsic and concentration risk. The credit risk of a bank's portfolio depends on both external and internal factors. The external factors are the state of the economy, wide swings in commodity/equity prices, foreign exchange rates and interest rates, trade restrictions, economic sanctions, government policies, etc. The internal factors are deficiencies in loan policies/administration, absence of prudential credit concentration limits, inadequately defined lending limits for loan officers/credit committees, deficiencies in appraisal of borrowers' financial position, excessive dependence on collaterals and inadequate risk pricing, absence of loan review mechanism and post-sanction surveillance, etc.

Another variant of credit risk is counterparty risk. The counterparty risk arises from non-performance of the trading partners. The non-performance may arise from counterparty's refusal/inability to perform due to adverse price movements or from external constraints that were not anticipated by the principal. The counterparty risk is generally viewed as a transient financial risk associated with trading rather than standard credit risk.

5.2 Sources of Credit Risk

Credit risk emanates from a banking institution's dealing with individuals, corporates, other banking institutions or a sovereign. For most banking institutions, loans are the largest and most obvious source of credit risk; however, credit risk could stem from activities both on- and off-balance sheet. Credit risk is most simply defined as the potential that a bank borrower or counterparty will fail to meet its obligations in accordance with the agreed terms. Credit risk is the likelihood that a debtor or financial instrument issuer is unwilling or unable to pay interest or repay the principal according to the terms specified in a credit agreement resulting in economic loss to the banking institution. Credit risk refers to the risk that a borrower will default on any type of debt by failing to make the required payments. The risk is primarily that of the lender and includes lost principal and interest, disruption to cash flows, and increased collection costs. The loss may be complete or partial and can arise in a number of circumstances. For example:

- A consumer may fail to make a payment due on a mortgage loan, credit loan, line of credit, or other loan.
- A company is unable to repay asset-secured fixed or floating charge debt.
- A business or consumer does not pay a trade invoice when due.
- A business does not pay an employee's earned wages when due.
- A business or government bond issuer does not make a payment on a coupon or principal payment when due.
- An insolvent insurance company does not pay a policy obligation.
- An insolvent bank does not return funds to a depositor.
- A government grants bankruptcy protection to an insolvent consumer or business.

To reduce the lender's credit risk, the lender may perform a credit check on the prospective borrower, may require the borrower to take out appropriate insurance, such as mortgage insurance or seek security or guarantees of third parties. In general, the higher the risk, the higher will be the interest rate that the debtor will be asked to pay on the debt.

According to the Basel Committee, "credit risk is most simply defined as the potential that a borrower or counterparty will fail to meet its obligations in accordance with the agreed terms". The Reserve Bank of India (RBI) has defined credit risk as "the probability of losses associated with diminution in the credit quality of borrowers or counterparties". Though credit risk is closely related with the business of lending i.e.

banks, it is in fact applicable to all activities where credit is involved (for example, manufacturers/traders sell their goods on credit to their customers).

5.3 Types of Credit Risk

Credit risk can be classified as follows:

5.3.1 Credit Default Risk: The risk of loss arising from a debtor being unlikely to pay its loan obligations in full or the debtor is more than 90 days past due on any material credit obligation; default risk may impact all credit-sensitive transactions, including loans, securities and derivatives.

5.3.2 Concentration Risk: The risk associated with any single exposure or group of exposures with the potential to produce large enough losses to threaten a bank's core operations. It may arise in the form of single name concentration or industry concentration.

5.3.3 Country Risk: The risk of loss arising from a sovereign state freezing foreign currency payments (transfer/conversion risk) or when it defaults on its obligations (sovereign risk); this type of risk is prominently associated with the country's macroeconomic performance and its political stability.

According to the Reserve Bank of India, the following are the forms of credit risk:

1. Non-payment of the principal of loan and/or the interest on it.
2. Contingent liabilities like letters of credit/guarantees issued by the bank on behalf of the client and upon crystallization amount not deposited by the customer.
3. In case of treasury operations, default by the counterparties in meeting the obligations.
4. In case of securities trading, settlement not taking place when it is due.
5. In the case of cross-border obligations, any default arising from the flow of foreign exchange and/or due to restrictions imposed on remittances out of the country.

However, the contributors to credit risk are: (i) credit corporate assets; (ii) retail assets; (iii) non-SLR portfolio; (iv) trading book and banking book; (v) inter-bank transactions; (vi) derivatives; and (vii) settlements etc.

One of the most important operations of a bank is lending money in the form of loans or giving credit. However, this operation generates certain risks. When any party approaches the bank for loans, the bank takes into account the following factors:

- **Probability of Default**: The possibility of failure to pay over the period stipulated in the contract and the computation for that year may be termed as the projected default rate.
- **Exposure of Credit**: How big of an amount will be the debt in case a default should occur?
- **Estimated Rate of Recovery**: What portion of the debt can be regained through freezing of assets and collateral and the like; should default transpire?

5.4 Components of Credit Risk

Credit risk is the risk that a borrower defaults and does not honour its obligation to service debt. It can occur when the counterpart is unable to pay or cannot pay on time. There can be many reasons for a default. In most cases, the obligor is in a financially stressed situation and may be facing a bankruptcy procedure. He can also refuse to comply with its debt service obligation, e.g., in the case of a fraud or a legal dispute. The loss in the case of default depends on the percentage that one can recover from the defaulted counterpart and the total exposure to the counterpart. A good risk manager tries to avoid large exposures on high-risk counterparts. In a banking institution's portfolio, losses also stem from reduction in portfolio value due to actual or perceived deterioration in credit quality. Thus, there are two components of credit risk:

1. **Default Risk:** Risk that a borrower or counterparty is unable to meet its commitment.
2. **Portfolio Risk:** That risk which arises from the

composition/concentration of bank's exposure to various factors.

Credit risk means that payments may be delayed or ultimately not paid at all, which can in turn cause cash flow problems and affect its liquidity. Credit risk is still the major single cause of bank failures. Credit risk consists of primarily two components, viz. quantity of risk, which is nothing but the outstanding loan balance as on the date of default and the quality of risk, viz. the severity of loss defined by both probability of default as reduced by the recoveries that could be made in the event of default. Thus, credit risk is a combined outcome of default risk and exposure risk. Credit risk consists of pre-settlement and settlement risk.

5.4.1 Pre-settlement Risk: Pre-settlement risk is the potential loss due to the counterpart's default during the life of the transaction (loan, bond, derivative product). Pre-settlement risk can exist over long periods, often years, starting from the time it is contracted until settlement. In addition to the counterpart default risk, there is also a risk that the counterpart is prohibited to pay when its country of domiciliation defaults and blocks all foreign payments. This risk is called sovereign transfer risk.

5.4.2 Settlement Risk: One is exposed to settlement risk because the payment or the exchange of cash flows is not made directly to the counterpart, but via one or multiple banks that may also default at the moment of the exchange. The risk is present as soon as an institution makes the required payment until the offsetting payment is received. The longer the time between the two payments, the higher is the risk. Large payments and payments in different time zones and in different currencies have a higher settlement risk. A major example of settlement risk was the failure of Herstatt Bank in Germany in 1974. Some of the money of payments that counterpart sent via the bank was not yet transferred to the recipients when the bank defaulted. One way to reduce settlement risk is by transferring only net amounts so that the amount exposed to settlement risk is reduced.

5.5 Approaches of Credit Risk

Banks always face the risk that some of its borrowers may default on repayment of loans, or interest on loan. This risk is called credit risk. Basel II norms require banks to accurately measure credit risk to hold sufficient capital to cover it. For the measurement of credit risk, Basel II framework prescribes three principal approaches for estimating capital charge to cover credit risk. The first option is the standardised (STD) approach and the second the internal-rating based (IRB) approach from which two variants exist, a foundation and an advanced IRB approach. The use of IRB approach is subject to an approval by the supervisors, based on standards established by the committee.

5.5.1 Standardized Approach: Under this approach, risk weight would be applied to each asset based on its external credit rating assigned by a rating agency. In each country, the regulator would approve the rating agencies in the country and decide on the applicable risk weight for each rating category. The framework proposes four risk weights viz. 20 percent, 50 percent, 100 percent and 150 percent. The framework provides the weights to be assigned for each of Standard & Poor's rating categories. For rating agencies in other countries, the regulator would be required to map the domestic rating agencies' ratings with those of S&P. In India, RBI has mapped Credit Rating Information Services of India Limited (CRISIL) and ICRA Ltd. (formerly, Investment Information and Credit Rating Agency of India Limited) ratings to those of Standard & Poor's (S&P) and has also prescribed risk weights for these ratings. The details of this mapping are set out in Table 5.1.

Table 5.1: Credit Risk: Standardized Approach

CRISIL/ICRA Rating	S&P Rating	Risk Weight (percent)
AAA	AAA to AA	20
AA	A+ to A	50
A	BBB+ to BB	100
BBB and below	Below BB	150
Unrated	Unrated	100

It is observed from the table that, asset with an investment grade rating of BBB from CRISIL or ICRA would carry a risk weight of 150 percent, which could lead to conservative estimates of capital requirement, especially for project finance loans. For retail portfolios, the framework provides for lower risk weights to account for the higher granularity and diversification effects embedded in these portfolios. As per the framework, the risk weight would be 35 percent for retail mortgages and 75 percent for all retail portfolios including mortgages. A risk weight of 100 percent means that an exposure is included in the calculation of risk weighted assets value, which translates into a capital charge equal to 9 percent of that value. GDCCB follows standardized approach to assess its credit risk.

5.5.2 Foundation Internal Rating Based Approach (Foundation IRB): In the foundation IRB approach, banks would internally estimate the probability of default (PD) for each rating category.

The estimate of loss given default (LGD) would be provided by the regulator. The framework provides a risk weight curve, which gives the risk weight for each combination of PD and LGD. A bank estimates each borrower's creditworthiness and the results are translated into estimates of a future potential loss amount, which form the basis of minimum capital requirements.

5.5.3 Advanced Internal Rating Based Approach (Advanced IRB): Under the advanced IRB approach, a bank with a sufficiently developed internal capital allocation process would be permitted to use its own inputs for estimation of potential future loss. Banks seeking to use this approach would need to have LGD and exposure at default (EAD) data history for at least seven years, in addition to meeting all the criteria stipulated for foundation IRB Approach. Under both IRB approaches, the range of risk weights is far more diverse than those in the STD approach, resulting in greater risk sensitivity.

5.6 Management of Credit Risk

Credit risk refers to the probability of loss due to a

borrower's failure to make payments on any type of debt. However, when the bank gets aggressive in its credit operations, such situations lead to credit risk and therefore it becomes important for the banks to do credit risk management. Credit risk is increasingly faced by banks in their product assortment (not only lending) and can be considered as the oldest and largest risk in banking. Important in a bank relationship is the "know your client principle", by becoming familiar with the borrower's credit base. It is important that banks deal with customers with sound reputation and creditworthiness. Therefore, banks need not only manage the credit risk in their credit portfolio but also in any individual credit transaction.

Credit risk management is undoubtedly among the most crucial issues in the field of financial risk management. With the recent financial turmoil and the regulatory changes introduced by Basel II, credit risk analysis and risk assessment in general have been receiving even greater attention by the financial and banking industry. The recent Basel II capital Accord articulates new market standards for credit risk management and capital adequacy for banks. The level of capital, a cushion to absorb credit and other losses, is matched to the portfolio risk depending on the risk characteristics of individual transactions, their concentration and correlation. All organizations, including banks, need to optimally allocate capital in relation to the selective investments made. Hence, efficient tools and techniques for risk measurement are a key cornerstone of a good credit risk management.

Credit risk management is the practice of mitigating the losses by understanding the adequacy of both a bank's capital and loan loss reserves at any given time—a process that has long been a challenge for financial institutions. The first step in effective credit risk management is to gain a complete understanding of a bank's overall credit risk by viewing risk at the individual, customer and portfolio levels. The philosophy behind it is that mostly all banks today practice credit risk management. They understand the importance of credit risk management and think of it as a ladder to growth by reducing their NPAs. Moreover, they are now using it as a tool to succeed over their competition because credit risk management practices reduce risk and improve return capital. Broadly, there are three causes for credit risk management.

1. Credit concentration.
2. Credit granting and/or monitoring process.
3. Credit exposure in the market and liquidity sensitivity sectors.

Generally speaking, credit risk is the largest source of risk, facing banking institutions. For these institutions, sound management involves measuring the credit risk at portfolio level to determine the amount of capital they need to hold as a cushion against potentially extreme losses. The goal of credit risk management is to maximise a bank's risk-adjusted rate of return by maintaining credit risk exposure within acceptable parameters. Banks need to manage the credit risk inherent in the entire portfolio as well as the risk in individual credits or transactions. Banks should also consider the relationships between credit risk and other risks. Effective credit risk management process is a way to manage portfolio of credit facilities.

Credit management is defined as the efficient control and co-ordination of loanable fund so as to keep credit and the investment in credit at optimal level. Credit risk management encompasses identification, measurement, monitoring and control of the credit risk exposures. The effective management of credit risk is a critical component of comprehensive risk management and essential for the long-term success of a banking organisation.

The management of credit risk should receive the top management's attention and the process should encompass:

- Measurement of risk through credit rating/scoring.
- Quantifying the risk through estimating expected loan losses i.e. the amount of loan losses that bank would

experience over a chosen time horizon (through tracking portfolio behaviour over 5 or more years) and unexpected loan losses i.e. the amount by which actual losses exceed the expected loss (through standard deviation of losses or the difference between expected loan losses and some selected target credit loss quintile).

- Risk pricing on a scientific basis.
- Controlling the risk through effective loan review mechanism and portfolio management.

Thus, for the requirements of effective credit risk management in banking, Basel II Accord identifies that effective credit risk management is a critical component of bank's overall risk management strategy and is essential to the long-term success of any banking organisation. Overall, the components of effective credit risk comprise of:

- Active board and senior management oversight.
- Sufficient policies, procedures and limits.
- Adequate risk measurement and monitoring.
- Management information systems.
- Comprehensive internal controls.

5.7 Principles for the Assessment of Banks' Management of Credit Risk

For most banks, loans are the largest and most obvious source of credit risk; however, other sources of credit risk exist throughout the activities of a bank, including in the banking book and in the trading book, and both on- and off-balance sheet. Banks are increasingly facing credit risk (or counterparty risk) in various financial instruments other than loans, including acceptances, inter-bank transactions, trade financing, foreign exchange transactions, financial futures, swaps, bonds, equities, options, and in the extension of commitments and guarantees, and the settlement of transactions.

As the goal of credit risk management is to maximise a bank's risk-adjusted rate of return by maintaining credit risk exposure within acceptable parameters, banks need to manage the credit risk inherent in the entire portfolio as well as the risk in individual credits or transactions. Banks should also consider the relationships between credit risk and other risks. The effective management of credit risk is a critical component of a comprehensive approach to risk management and essential for the long-term success of any banking organisation. Basel Committee on Banking Supervision has issued broad guidelines for best practices in credit risk management.

5.7.1 Appropriate Credit Risk Environment:

Principle 1: The board of directors should have responsibility for approving and periodically (at least annually) reviewing the credit risk strategy and significant credit risk policies of the bank. The strategy should reflect the bank's tolerance for risk and the level of profitability the bank expects to achieve for incurring various credit risks.

Principle 2: Senior management should have responsibility for implementing the credit risk strategy approved by the board of directors and for developing policies and procedures for identifying, measuring, monitoring and controlling the credit risk. Such policies and procedures should address credit risk in all of the bank's activities and at both the individual credit and portfolio levels.

Principle 3: Banks should identify and manage credit risk inherent in all products and activities. Banks should ensure that the risks of products and activities new to them are subject to adequate risk management procedures and controls before being introduced or undertaken, and approved in advance by the board of directors or its appropriate committee.

5.7.2 Operating under a Sound Credit Granting Process:

Principle 4: Banks must operate within sound, well-defined credit granting criteria. These criteria should include a clear indication of the bank's target market and a thorough understanding of the borrower or counterparty, as well as the purpose and structure of the credit, and its source of repayment.

Principle 5: Banks should establish overall credit limits at the level of individual borrowers and counterparties, and groups of connected counterparties that aggregate in a comparable and meaningful manner with different types of exposures, both in the banking and trading book and on and off the balance sheet.

Principle 6: Banks should have a clearly-established process in place for approving new credits as well as the amendment, renewal and re-financing of existing credits.

Principle 7: All extensions of credit must be made on an arm's-length basis. In particular, credits to related companies and individuals must be authorised on an exception basis, monitored with particular care and other appropriate steps taken to control or mitigate the risks of non-arm's length lending.

5.7.3 Maintaining an Appropriate Credit Administration, Measurement and Monitoring Process:

Principle 8: Banks should have in place a system for the ongoing administration of their various credit risk-bearing portfolios.

Principle 9: Banks must have in place a system for monitoring the condition of individual credits, including determining the adequacy of provisions and reserves.

Principle 10: Banks are encouraged to develop and utilise an internal risk rating system in managing credit risk. The rating system should be consistent with the nature, size and complexity of a bank's activities.

Principle 11: Banks must have information systems and analytical techniques that enable management to measure the credit risk inherent in all on- and off-balance sheet activities. The management information system should provide adequate information on the composition of the credit portfolio, including identification of any concentrations of risk.

Principle 12: Banks must have in place a system for monitoring the overall composition and quality of the credit portfolio.

Principle 13: Banks should take into consideration potential future changes in economic conditions when assessing individual credits and their credit portfolios, and should assess their credit risk exposures under stressful conditions.

5.7.4 Ensuring Adequate Controls over Credit Risk:

Principle 14: Banks must establish a system of independent, ongoing assessment of the bank's credit risk management processes and the results of such reviews should be communicated directly to the board of directors and senior management.

Principle 15: Banks must ensure that the credit-granting function is being properly managed and that credit exposures are within levels consistent with prudential standards and internal limits. Banks should establish and enforce internal controls and other practices to ensure that exceptions to policies, procedures and limits are reported in a timely manner to the appropriate level of management for action.

Principle 16: Banks must have a system in place for early remedial action on deteriorating credits, problem credits and similar workout situations.

5.7.5 Role of Supervisors:

Principle 17: Supervisors should ensure that banks have an effective system in place to identify, measure, monitor and control credit risk as part of an overall approach to risk management. Supervisors should conduct an independent evaluation of a bank's strategies, policies, procedures and practices related to the granting of credit and the ongoing management of the portfolio. Supervisors should consider setting prudential limits to restrict bank exposures to single borrowers or groups of connected counterparties.

5.8 Tools of Credit Risk Management

Credit risk management encompasses a host of management techniques, which help the banks in mitigating the adverse impacts of credit risk. For this, there is a need to understand the basic concepts for measuring credit risk which includes probability of default, recovery rate, exposure at default, expected loss, loss given default, and unexpected loss. The instruments and tools, through which credit risk management is carried out, are detailed below.

5.8.1 Credit Approving Authority: Multi-tier credit approving authority, constitution-wise delegation of powers, higher delegated powers for better-rated customers, discriminatory time schedule for review/renewal, hurdle rates and benchmarks for fresh exposures and periodicity for renewal based on risk rating, etc. should be formulated. Each bank should have a carefully formulated scheme of delegation of powers.

The banks should also evolve multi-tier credit approving system where the loan proposals are approved by an 'approval grid' or a 'committee'. The credit facilities above a specified limit may be approved by the 'grid' or 'committee', comprising at least 3 to 4 officers and invariably one officer should represent the CRMD, who has no volume and profit targets. Banks can also consider credit approving committees at various operating levels i.e. large branches (where considered necessary), regional offices, zonal offices, head offices, etc. Banks could consider delegating powers for sanction of higher limits to the 'approval grid' or the 'committee' for better rated/quality customers. The spirit of the credit approving system may be that no credit proposals should be approved or recommended to higher authorities, if majority members of the 'approval grid' or 'committee' do not agree on the creditworthiness of the borrower. In case of disagreement, the specific views of the dissenting member/s should be recorded.

The banks should also evolve suitable framework for reporting and evaluating the quality of credit decisions taken by various functional groups. The quality of credit decisions should be evaluated within a reasonable time, say 3-6 months, through a well-defined loan review mechanism.

5.8.2 Prudential Limits: In order to limit the magnitude of credit risk, prudential limits should be laid down on various aspects of credit:

1. Stipulate benchmark current/debt equity and profitability ratios, debt service coverage ratio or other ratios, with flexibility for deviations. The conditions subject to which deviations are permitted and the authority therefore should also be clearly spelt out in the loan policy.
2. Single/group borrower limits, which may be lower than the limits prescribed by the Reserve Bank to provide a filtering mechanism.
3. Substantial exposure limit i.e. sum total of exposures assumed in respect of those single borrowers enjoying credit facilities in excess of a threshold limit, say 10 percent or 15 percent of the capital funds. The substantial exposure limit may be fixed at 600 percent or 800 percent of capital funds, depending upon the degree of concentration risk, the bank is exposed to.
4. Maximum exposure limits to industry, sector, etc. should be set up. There must also be systems in place to evaluate the exposures at reasonable intervals and the limits should be adjusted especially when a particular sector or industry faces slowdown or other sector/industry specific problems. The exposure limits to sensitive sectors, such as, advances against equity shares, real estate, etc., which are subject to a high degree of asset price volatility and to specific industries, which are subject to frequent business cycles, may necessarily be restricted. Similarly, high-risk industries, as perceived by the bank, should also be placed under lower portfolio limit. Any excess exposure should be fully backed by adequate collaterals or strategic considerations.
5. Banks may consider maturity profile of the loan book, keeping in view the market risks inherent in the balance sheet, risk evaluation capability, liquidity etc.

Prudential limit is linked to capital funds, say 15 percent

for individual borrower entity and 40 percent for a group with additional 10 percent for infrastructure projects undertaken by the group. Threshold limit is fixed at a level lower than prudential exposure. Substantial exposure, which is the sum total of the exposures beyond the threshold limit, should not exceed 600 percent to 800 percent of the capital funds of the bank (i.e. six to eight times).

5.8.3 Risk Rating: Rating implies an assessment or evaluation of a person, property, project or affairs against a specific yardstick/benchmark set for the purpose. In credit rating, the objective is to assess/evaluate a particular credit proposition (which includes investment) on the basis of certain parameters. The outcome indicates the degree of credit reliability and risk. The Basel Committee has defined credit rating as a summary indicator of the risk inherent in an individual credit, embodying an assessment of the risk of loss due to the default counterparty, by considering relevant quantitative and qualitative information. Thus, credit rating is a tool for the measurement or quantification of credit risk.

Banks should have a comprehensive risk scoring/rating system that serves as a single point indicator of diverse risk factors of a counterparty and for taking credit decisions in a consistent manner. To facilitate this, a substantial degree of standardisation is required in ratings across borrowers. The risk rating system should be designed to reveal the overall risk of lending, critical input for setting pricing and non-price terms of loans as also present meaningful information for review and management of loan portfolio. The risk rating, in short, should reflect the underlying credit risk of the loan book. The rating exercise should also facilitate the credit granting authorities, some comfort in its knowledge of loan quality at any moment of time. The risk rating system should be drawn up in a structured manner. Banks may also consider separate rating framework for large corporate/small borrowers, traders, etc. that exhibit varying nature and degree of the risk.

Further, as a prudent risk management policy, each bank

should prescribe the minimum rating below which no exposures would be undertaken. Any flexibility in the minimum standards and conditions for relaxation and authority there for, should be clearly articulated in the loan policy. The credit risk assessment exercise should be repeated biannually (or even at shorter intervals for low quality customers) and should be delinked invariably from the regular renewal exercise.

The updating of the credit ratings should be undertaken normally at quarterly intervals or at least at half-yearly intervals, in order to gauge the quality of the portfolio at periodic intervals. Variations in the ratings of borrowers over time indicate changes in credit quality and expected loan losses from the credit portfolio.

Thus, if the rating system is to be meaningful, the credit quality reports should signal changes in expected loan losses. In order to ensure the consistency and accuracy of internal ratings, the responsibility for setting or confirming such ratings should vest with the loan review function and examined by an independent loan review group. The banks should undertake comprehensive study on migration (upward, i.e. lower to higher and downward, i.e. higher to lower) of borrowers in the ratings to add accuracy in expected loan loss calculations.

5.8.4 Risk Pricing: Banks should build historical database on the portfolio quality and provisioning/charge off to equip themselves to price the risk. But value of collateral, market forces, perceived value of accounts, future business potential, portfolio/industry exposure and strategic reasons may also play important role in pricing. Risk-return pricing is a fundamental tenet of risk management. In a risk-return setting, borrowers with weak financial position and hence placed in high credit risk category should be priced high.

Thus, banks should evolve scientific systems to price the credit risk, which should have a bearing on the expected probability of default. The pricing of loans normally should be linked to risk rating or credit quality. The probability of default could be derived from the past behaviour of the loan portfolio, which is the function of loan loss provision/charge offs for the last five years or so. Large sized banks across the world have already put in place risk adjusted return on capital (RAROC) framework for pricing of loans, which calls for data on portfolio behaviour and allocation of capital, commensurate with credit risk inherent in loan proposals. Under RAROC framework, lender begins by charging an interest mark-up to cover the expected loss, i.e. expected default rate of the rating category of the borrower. The lender then allocates enough capital to the prospective loan borrower to cover some amount of unexpected loss variability of default rates.

5.8.5 Portfolio Management: The need for credit portfolio management emanates from the necessity to optimize the benefits associated with diversification and to reduce the potential adverse impact of concentration of exposures to a particular borrower, sector or industry. There is a need to stipulate quantitative ceiling on aggregate exposure on specific rating categories, distribution of borrowers in various industry, business group and conduct of rapid portfolio reviews. Credit control and monitoring at portfolio level deals with the risk of a given portfolio, expected losses, requirement of risk capital, and impact of changing the portfolio mix on risk, expected losses and capital. Banks should evolve proper systems for identification of credit weaknesses well in advance.

The existing framework of tracking the non-performing loans around the balance sheet date does not signal the quality of the entire loan book. Most international banks have adopted various portfolio management techniques for gauging asset quality. The CRMD, set up at head office should be assigned the responsibility of periodic monitoring of the portfolio. The portfolio quality could be evaluated by tracking the migration (upward or downward) of borrowers from one rating scale to another. This process would be meaningful only if the borrower-wise ratings are updated at quarterly/half-yearly intervals. Data on movements within grading categories provide a useful insight into the nature and composition of loan book. The banks could also consider the following measures to maintain the portfolio quality:

1. Stipulate quantitative ceiling on aggregate exposure in specified rating categories, i.e. certain percentage of total advances should be in the rating category of 1 to 2 or 1 to 3, 2 to 4 or 4 to 5 etc.
2. Evaluate the rating-wise distribution of borrowers in various industry, business segments, etc.
3. Exposure to one industry/sector should be evaluated on the basis of overall rating distribution of borrowers in the sector/group. In this context, banks should weigh the pros and cons of specialisation and concentration by industry group. In cases where portfolio exposure to a single industry is badly performing, the banks may increase the quality standards for that specific industry.
4. Target rating-wise volume of loans, probable defaults and provisioning requirements as a prudent planning exercise. For any deviation/s from the expected parameters, an exercise for restructuring of the portfolio should immediately be undertaken and if necessary, the entry level criteria could be enhanced to insulate the portfolio from further deterioration.
5. Undertake rapid portfolio reviews, stress tests and scenario analysis when external environment undergoes rapid changes (e.g. volatility in the forex market, economic sanctions, changes in the fiscal/monetary policies, general slowdown of the economy, market risk events, extreme liquidity conditions, etc.). The stress tests would reveal undetected areas of potential credit risk exposure and linkages between different categories of risk. In adverse circumstances, there may be substantial correlation of various risks, especially credit and market risks. Stress testing can range from relatively simple alterations in assumptions about one or more financial, structural or economic variables to the use of highly sophisticated

models. The output of such portfolio-wide stress tests should be reviewed by the board and suitable changes may be made in prudential risk limits for protecting the quality. Stress tests could also include contingency plans, detailing management responses to stressful situations.

6. Introduce discriminatory time schedules for renewal of borrower limits. Lower rated borrowers whose financials show signs of problems should be subjected to renewal control twice/thrice a year.

Many of the international banks have adopted credit risk models for evaluation of credit portfolio. The credit risk models offer banks, framework for examining credit risk exposures across geographical locations and product lines in a timely manner, centralising data and analysing marginal and absolute contributions to risk. J.P. Morgan has developed a portfolio model 'Credit Metrics' for evaluating credit risk. The model basically focuses on estimating the volatility in the value of assets caused by variations in the quality of assets. The volatility is computed by tracking the probability that the borrower might migrate from one rating category to another (downgrade or upgrade). Thus, the value of loans can change over time, reflecting migration of the borrowers to a different risk-rating grade. The model can be used for promoting transparency in credit risk, establishing benchmark for credit risk measurement and estimating economic capital for credit risk under the RAROC framework.

5.8.6 Loan Review Mechanism (LRM): LRM is an effective tool for constantly evaluating the quality of loan book and to bring about qualitative improvements in credit administration. Banks should, therefore, put in place proper loan review mechanism for large value accounts with responsibilities assigned in various areas such as, evaluating the effectiveness of loan administration, maintaining the integrity of credit grading process, assessing the loan loss provision, portfolio quality, etc. The complexity and scope of LRM normally varies, based on banks' size, type of operations and management practices. It should target all loans above certain cut-off limit ensuring that at least 30 percent to 40 percent of the portfolio is subjected to LRM in a year so as to ensure that all major credit risks embedded in the balance sheet have been tracked.

It may be independent of the CRMD or even separate department in large banks. Accurate and timely credit grading is one of the basic components of an effective LRM. Credit grading involves assessment of credit quality, identification of problem loans, and assignment of risk ratings. Banks should formulate loan review policy and it should be reviewed annually by the board. It may be independent of the CRMD or even separate department in large banks.

The main objectives of LRM could be:

- To identify promptly, loans which develop credit weaknesses and initiate timely corrective action;
- To evaluate portfolio quality and isolate potential problem areas;
- To provide information for determining adequacy of loan loss provision;
- To assess the adequacy of and adherence to, loan policies and procedures, and to monitor compliance with relevant laws and regulations; and
- To provide top management with information on credit administration, including credit sanction process, risk evaluation and post-sanction follow-up.

Accurate and timely credit grading is one of the basic components of an effective LRM. Credit grading involves assessment of credit quality, identification of problem loans, and assignment of risk ratings. A proper credit grading system should support evaluating the portfolio quality and establishing loan loss provisions. Given the importance and subjective nature of credit rating, the credit ratings awarded by credit administration department should be subjected to review by loan review officers who are independent of loan administration. Banks should formulate loan review policy and it should be reviewed annually by the board. The policy should, *inter alia*, address:

1. The loan review officers should have sound knowledge in credit appraisal, lending practices and loan policies of the bank. They should also be well versed in the relevant laws/regulations that affect lending activities. The independence of loan review officers should be ensured and the findings of the reviews should also be reported directly to the board or committee of the board.
2. The loan reviews are designed to provide feedback on effectiveness of credit sanction and to identify incipient deterioration in portfolio quality. Reviews of high value loans should be undertaken usually within three months of sanction/renewal or more frequently when factors indicate a potential for deterioration in the credit quality. The scope of the review should cover all loans above a cut-off limit. In addition, banks should also target other accounts that present elevated risk characteristics. At least 30-40 percent of the portfolio should be subjected to LRM in a year to provide reasonable assurance that all the major credit risks embedded in the balance sheet have been tracked.
3. The loan reviews should focus on: (a) approval process, (b) accuracy and timeliness of credit ratings assigned by loan officers, (c) adherence to internal policies and procedures and applicable laws, (d) compliance with loan covenants, (e) post-sanction follow-up, (f) sufficiency of loan documentation, (g) portfolio quality, and (h) recommendations for improving portfolio quality.

The findings of reviews should be discussed with line managers and the corrective actions should be elicited for all deficiencies. Deficiencies that remain unresolved should be reported to the top management.

5.9 Credit Derivatives

The credit derivatives are gaining increasing popularity in many countries. Since the early 1990s, there has been proliferation of different types of credit derivatives in several countries.

A credit derivative is a contract (derivative) to transfer the risk of the total return on a credit asset falling below an agreed level, without transfer of the underlying asset. This is usually achieved by transferring risk on a credit reference asset. Early forms of credit derivatives were financial guarantees. Credit derivatives are designed to allow independent trading/hedging of credit risk. It is also possible to transfer and/or transform credit risk through securitisation. Credit derivative is a logical extension of two of the most significant developments in financial markets, viz., securitisation and derivatives.

5.9.1 Forms of Credit Derivatives: Credit derivatives are instruments that transfer a part or all of the credit risk of an obligation (or a pool of obligations), without transferring the ownership of the underlying asset(s). This is usually achieved by transferring risk on a credit reference asset. Three common forms of credit derivatives are credit default swap (CDS), total return swap (TRS) and credit linked note (CLN).

A. Credit Default Swap (CDS): A CDS consists of swapping, usually on an ongoing basis, the risk premium inherent in an interest rate on a bond or a loan in return for a cash payment that is made in the event of default by the debtor. The CDS has become the main driver of the credit derivatives market, offering liquid price discovery and trading on which the rest of the market is based. It is an agreement between a protection buyer and a protection seller, whereby the buyer pays a periodic fee in return for a contingent payment by the seller upon a credit event happening in the reference entity. The contingent payment usually replicates the loss incurred by creditor of the reference entity in the event of its default. It covers only the credit risk embedded in the asset. Risks arising from other factors, such as interest rate movements, remain with the buyer.

B. Total Return Swap (TRS): A TRS (also known as total rate of return swap) is a contract between two counterparties, whereby they swap periodic payments for the period of the contract. Typically, one party receives the total return (interest payments plus any capital gains or losses for the payment period) from a specified reference asset, while the other receives a specified fixed or floating cash flow that is not related to the creditworthiness of the reference asset, as with a vanilla interest rate swap. The payments are based upon the same notional amount. The reference asset may be any asset, index or basket of assets. The TRS is simply a mechanism that allows one party to derive the economic benefit of owning an asset without use of the balance sheet, and which allows the other to effectively buy protection against loss in value due to ownership of a credit asset.

While the CDS provides protection against specific credit events, the TRS protects against the loss of value irrespective of cause—whether default and widening of credit spreads—among others.

C. Credit Linked Note (CLN): A CLN is an instrument whose cash flow depends upon a credit event, which can be a default, credit spread, or a rating change. The definition of the relevant credit events must be negotiated by the parties to the note. A CLN, in effect, combines a credit-default swap with a regular note (with coupon, maturity, redemption). Given its regular note features, a CLN is an on-balance sheet asset, unlike a CDS.

5.9.2 Significance of Credit Derivatives: Credit derivative markets are most active where credit quality measurement and rating systems are transparent and have widespread adoption as in North America and Europe. In addition, the demand for structured credit products in Asia and the Middle East has been growing. The rapid pace of growth and widespread participation in the credit derivatives market in several countries has transformed the financial landscape. Credit derivatives have significance for both banks and investors in mitigating credit risk. For instance, a commercial bank can use credit derivatives to manage the risk of its loan portfolio and an investment bank can use credit derivatives to manage the risks it incurs when underwriting securities. Investors—such as an insurance company, asset manager, or hedge fund—can use credit derivatives to align its credit risk exposure with its desired credit risk profile.

Credit derivatives in international markets have effectively helped to enhance the efficiency of the financial system by providing to both banks and non-banking financial institutions, access to a broader range of risk-return combinations and a wider pool of underlying risks and enhancing the liquidity of corporate bond markets. The information revealed through credit derivative mechanism is very useful for supervision and market surveillance.

5.9.3 Benefits of Credit Derivatives: Banks and financial institutions derive at least three main benefits from credit derivatives:

1. Credit derivatives allow banks to transfer credit risk and hence free up capital, which can be used for other productive purposes.
2. Banks can conduct business on existing client relationships in excess of exposure norms and transfer away the risks. For instance, a bank which has hit its exposure limits with a client group may have to turn down a lucrative guarantee deal. However, with credit derivatives, the bank can take up the guarantee and maintain its exposure limits by transferring the credit risk on the guarantee or previous exposures. This allows banks to maintain client relationships.
3. Banks can construct and manage a credit risk portfolio of their own choice and risk appetite, unconstrained by funds, distribution and sales effort.

5.9.4 Risks Involved in Credit Derivatives: Credit derivatives pose risk management challenges of their own. Credit derivatives can transform credit risk in intricate ways that may not be easy to understand. Complex credit derivatives rely on complex models, leading to model risk. Credit rating agencies interpret this complexity for investors, but their ratings can be misunderstood, creating rating agency risk. The settlement of a credit derivative contract following a default can have its own complications, creating settlement risk. Apart from these risks, the credit risk remains the core risk in the credit derivative segment.

The use of credit derivative instruments has changed the underlying borrower-lender relationship and established new relationships between lenders that become risk shedders and the new risk takers. This new relationship has the potential for market failure due, for instance, to asymmetric information. The growth of hedge funds, particularly credit-oriented hedge funds, has accelerated market development and credit risk dispersion. While credit derivative markets increasingly facilitate the primary transfer of credit risk, secondary market liquidity is still lacking within some segments, creating the potential for market disruptions. As such, these markets are subject to increased attention from supervisors and policymakers and raise some supervisory concerns.

In short, the use of credit derivatives raises the following concerns:

1. Some of the credit derivatives, which are being used, are at their infancy and need to mature. Introduction of such products, therefore, may be potentially destabilising.
2. The measurement and management of credit risk is much more complicated than market risk.
3. Documentation risk is an important aspect of credit derivatives.
4. Certain incentive issues arise with the use of credit derivatives. This is because such instruments typically change the underlying borrower-lender relationship and establish new relationships between lenders that become risk shedders and the new risk takers. This new relationship has the potential for market failure due, for instance, to asymmetric information.

5.9.5 Credit Derivatives and Sub-prime Crisis of 2007: The role that credit derivatives played in the 2007 sub-prime crisis is well-known. The macroeconomic environment with a prolonged period of low interest rates, high liquidity and low volatility led to underestimation of risks by financial institutions, breakdown of credit and risk management practices in many financial institutions, and shortcomings in financial regulation and supervision. Banks, especially in the US, increasingly turned to *originate and distribute model* in which they bundled and sold standardised mortgages as securities. Though favourable credit ratings were obtained for most of these bundled securities by carefully structuring their priority in receiving cash flow from servicing of the original portfolio, many of these were in reality, sub-prime securities. As housing prices in the US declined, the defaults rose in several leading international banks. The kind of problems witnessed in the US sub-prime mortgage market can also surface in other types of lending such as leveraged loans and consumer credit. Furthermore, such problems may not be confined to industrial countries, but can surface in other emerging economies as well where financial institutions take excessive risks in the wake of weak lending practices, and where regulatory and supervisory frameworks are found to be inadequate.

The unbridled proliferation of complex credit derivatives and excessive risk transfer by adoption of the originate-to-distribute model is recognised as one of the root causes of the current financial crisis. The recent credit turmoil has also underscored the importance of liquidity risk arising from off-balance sheet commitments—implicit or explicit—of the credit intermediaries.

While the development of markets for credit derivatives and asset securitization products can play a critical role in furthering economic growth, this requires to be pursued in a gradual manner by sequencing reforms and putting in place appropriate safeguards before introducing such products.

5.9.6 Credit Derivatives in India: The credit market refers to the market where financial instruments that embrace credit risk are traded. In addition to traditional instruments, such as loans and advances, corporate bonds, and commercial papers, the credit market now includes securitised products in which various credit risks have been pooled as well as credit derivatives whose underlying assets encompass credit risks.

As a financial system which is dominated by bank intermediation, credit has traditionally been the main source of funds to various sectors in the Indian economy, and loans and advances continue to be the preferred part cf the asset books of the banks. However, the implementation of risk management guidelines and the requirement for providing a capital charge for credit risk in the balance sheet has given banks an incentive to look for innovative methods of transferring credit risk from their books.

While simple techniques for transferring credit risk, such as financial guarantees, collateral and credit insurance have long been prevalent in the Indian banking industry, the recent innovative instruments in credit risk transfer are yet to make an impact. However, in recent years the risk management architecture of banks in India has strengthened and they are on the way to becoming Basel II compliant, providing adequate comfort level for the introduction of credit derivatives.

The Reserve Bank in its Annual Policy announced in April 2007 mentioned that as part of the gradual process of financial sector liberalization in India, it was considered appropriate to introduce credit derivatives in a calibrated manner. Furthermore, the amendment to the Reserve Bank of India Act, 1934 had provided legality to OTC (over the counter) derivative instruments, including credit derivatives.

Although derivative instruments were introduced in July 1999 in the money/foreign exchange market in the form of forward rate agreements (FRAs) and interest rate swaps (IRS), credit derivatives are yet to be introduced. The RBI's Annual Policy Statement 2007-08 announced the introduction of credit derivatives in India in a calibrated manner. In view of certain adverse developments in the international financial markets, especially credit markets, resulting from recent financial turmoil, it was widely felt that time is not opportune to introduce the credit derivatives in India for the present. As such, the RBI announced on June 19, 2008 its decision to keep in abeyance the issuance of the final guidelines on introduction of credit derivatives in India.

6

Risk Regulations in Banks: Basel Norms

Banks are the backbone of an economy and a strong banking system is a must for any economy to function smoothly and to prosper. As it is already seen that banks face many risks and if risks are not properly regulated, banks may fail and the effect of such failure on an economy would be disastrous. Regulations have decisive impact on risk management. They set up the constraints and guidelines that inspire risk management practices and helps in developing the risk management processes of banks. Regulations helps in: (i) improving the safety of the banks by imposing capital requirements in line with bank's risks, (ii) promoting sound business and supervisory practices, (iii) controlling and monitoring 'systematic risk', (iv) protecting interest of depositors as depositors cannot impose a real market discipline on banks and, (v) levelling the competitive playing field of banks by setting common benchmarks for all players.

6.1 Systematic Risk

Systematic risk is the risk of failure of the whole banking system. In fact, it is a major challenge for the regulator because the failure of a single bank generates a risk of failure for all banks that have ongoing commitments with the defaulting bank. And an individual bank's failure is one of the major sources of this risk.

Systematic risk is the risk of asset value change associated with systematic factors. It is sometimes referred to as *market risk*, which is in fact a somewhat imprecise term. By its nature, this risk can be hedged, but cannot be diversified completely. In fact, systematic risk can be thought of as undiversifiable risk. All investors assume this type of risk, whenever assets owned or claims issued are subject to change in value as a result of broad economic factors. As such, systematic risk comes in many different forms. For the banking sector, however, two are of greatest concern, namely variations in the general level of interest rates and the relative value of currencies.

Because of the bank's dependence on these systematic factors, most try to estimate the impact of these particular systematic risks on performance, attempt to hedge against them and thus limit the sensitivity to variations in undiversifiable factors. Accordingly, most will track *interest rate risk* closely. They measure and manage the firm's vulnerability to interest rate variation, even though they cannot do so perfectly.

A number of factors helped stabilize the banking system. Regulatory environment is a necessity for risk control in banks. Deregulation in an economy came in to promote growth, as a regulated environment hardly provides any incentive for competition and change. Deregulation increased competition between players unprepared by their past experiences, thereby resulting in increasing risks for the system and is translated in several failures. Even competition promoted globalization that resulted in cross-country transactions. Hence, Basel Committee on Banking Supervision (BCBS) undertook regulatory framework for reconciling risk control.

The Reserve Bank of India, the central bank and the chief regulator of the banking system in India, were conscious of the ever increasing dimensions of various risks faced by the banking system in India and have been initiating steps in this directions. And also from 1965 to 1981 there were about eight bank failures (or bankruptcies) in the United States. Bank failures were particularly prominent during the 1980s, a time which is usually referred to as the "savings and loan crisis". Banks throughout the world were lending extensively, while countries' external indebtedness was growing at an unsustainable rate.

As a result, the potential for bankruptcy of the major

international banks grew as a result of low security. In order to prevent this risk, the Basel Committee on Banking Supervision, comprised of central banks and supervisory authorities of 10 countries, met in 1987 in Basel, Switzerland.

The Committee drafted a first document to set up an international 'minimum' amount of capital that banks should hold. This minimum is a percentage of the total capital of a bank, which is also called the minimum risk-based capital adequacy. The Basel Committee is the primary global standard-setter for the prudential regulation of banks and provides a forum for cooperation on banking supervisory matters. Its mandate is to strengthen the regulation, supervision and practices of banks worldwide with the purpose of enhancing financial stability. The Committee reports to the Group of Governors and Heads of Supervision (GHOS). The Committee seeks the endorsement of GHOS for its major decisions and its work programme.

Under the aegis of Bank for International Settlements (BIS), bankers met at Basel situated in Switzerland to address the common issues concerning bankers all over the world. The Basel Committee on Banking Supervision (BCBS) is a committee of banking supervisory authorities that was established by the central bank governors of the Group of Ten countries in 1974. It provides a forum for regular cooperation on banking supervisory matters. Its objective is to enhance understanding of key supervisory issues and improve the quality of banking supervision worldwide.

The Committee is staffed mainly by professional supervisors on temporary basis from member institutions. In addition to undertaking the secretarial work for the Committee and its many expert sub-committees, it stands ready to give advice to supervisory authorities in all countries. The Basel Committee on Banking Supervision (BCBS) is a committee of banking supervisory authorities of G-10 countries and has been developing standards and establishment of a framework for bank supervision towards strengthening financial stability throughout the world. In consultation with the supervisory authorities of a few non-G-10 countries including India, core principles for effective banking supervision in the form of minimum requirements to strengthen current supervisory regime, were mooted.

In 1988, the Basel I Capital Accord (agreement) was created. The Basel II Capital Accord follows as an extension of the former, and was implemented in 2007. The 1988 Capital Accord essentially provided only one option for measuring the appropriate capital in relation to the risk-weighted assets of the financial institution. It focused on the total amount of bank capital so as to reduce the risk of bank solvency at the potential cost of bank's failure for the depositors.

Prudential norms include controls imposed by the central bank on activities of banks. The concept of risk management in Indian context was proposed by Narasimham Committee (1991) on Financial Sector Reforms which pointed out the capital adequacy requirement and risk constraints by devising necessary prudential norms by RBI. Jehan *et al.* (2010) note that consequent upon the recommendations of the Narasimham Committee, a capital adequacy ratio (CAR), also known as capital to risk weighted assets ratio (CRAR) system was introduced for banks in India from April 1992, largely in conformity with international standards. The Report had advised the minimum CRAR at 8 percent for all commercial banks and provisions of penalty for the banks that could not maintain it. These prudential norms were recommended to meet revised Basel I standards. However, these norms are generally endorsed by RBI to suit Indian situation.

6.2 Basel I Norms

In 1988, the Basel I Capital Accord was created. The general purpose was to:

1. Strengthen the stability of international banking system.
2. Set up a fair and a consistent international banking system in order to decrease competitive inequality among

international banks.

Basel I primarily focused on credit risk. The assets of banks were classified and grouped into five categories according to credit risk, carrying risk weights of zero (e.g. home country sovereign debts), 10, 20, 50, and up to 100 percent (for corporate debts). Banks with international presence were required to hold capital equal to 8 percent of the risk-weighted assets. This framework for capital adequacy was designed to establish minimum levels of capital for internationally active banks. However, its simplicity encouraged over 100 countries across the world to not only adopt the framework but also apply it across the entire banking segment without restricting it to the internationally active banks.

The basic achievement of Basel I has been to define bank capital and the so-called bank capital ratio. In order to set up a minimum risk-based capital adequacy applying to all banks and governments in the world, a general definition of capital was required. Indeed, before this international agreement, there was no single definition of bank capital. The first step of the agreement was thus to define it.

6.2.1 Two-Tiered Capital

Based on the Basel norms, the RBI also issued similar capital adequacy norms for the Indian banks. According to these guidelines, the banks will have to identify their Tier-I and Tier-II capital and assign risk weights to the assets. Having done this, they will have to assess the capital to risk weighted assets ratio (CRAR).

A. Tier-I Capital (Core Capital)

1. Paid-up capital.
2. Statutory reserves.
3. Disclosed free reserves.
4. Capital reserves representing surplus arising out of sale proceeds of assets.
5. Equity investments in subsidiaries, intangible assets and losses in the current period and those brought forward from previous periods will be deducted from Tier-I capital.

B. Tier-II Capital (Supplementary Capital)

1. Undisclosed reserves and cumulative perpetual preference shares.
2. Revaluation reserves.
3. General provisions and loss reserves.

In other words, CAR is ratio of capital fund to risk weighted assets expressed as a percentage. Having done this they will have to assess the CAR. The minimum CAR which the Indian banks are required to meet is set at 9 percent. CAR is expressed as a percentage of a bank's risk-weighted credit exposure. Formally, CAR =Tier-1 capital + Tier-2 capital/risk weighted assets.

CAR is generally arrived at by taking into account the loan type and its risk-proneness. Higher the risk, higher will be the CAR and vice-versa. This ratio keeps changing as banks may vary their loan type from time to time. Similarly, a certain percentage of risk-weighted assets are allocated for a particular loan type which may not be fully used. In any case, the CAR is fixed by the management, taking into account the market condition for each type of loan. Hence, CAR is an amalgam of credit, operational and market risks. As a consequence, the CAR varies during a given financial year.

Credit risk is defined as the risk weighted asset (RWA) of the bank, which are bank's assets weighted in relation to their relative credit risk levels. According to Basel I, the total capital should represent at least 8 percent of the bank's credit risk (RWA). In addition, the Basel agreement identifies three types of credit risks:

1. The on-balance sheet risk.
2. The trading off-balance sheet risk. These are derivatives, namely interest rates, foreign exchange, equity derivatives and commodities.
3. The non-trading off-balance sheet risk. These include general guarantees, such as forward purchase of assets or transaction-related debt assets.

The Basel I Capital Accord aimed to assess capital in relation to credit risk, or the risk that a loss will occur if a party does not fulfil its obligations. It focused almost entirely on credit risk (default risk)—the risk of counterparty failure. It defined capital requirement and structure of risk weights for banks. Basel I, as the first international instrument assessing the importance of risk in relation to capital, will remain a milestone in the finance and banking history.

6.2.2 Advantages of Basel I:

1. Substantial increases in capital adequacy ratios of internationally active banks.
2. Relatively simple structure.
3. Worldwide adoption.
4. Increased competitive equality among internationally active banks.
5. Greater discipline in managing capital.
6. A benchmark for assessment by market participants.

6.2.3 Weaknesses of Basel I:

In spite of advantages and positive effects, weaknesses of Basel I standards eventually became evident:

1. Capital adequacy depends on credit risk, while other risks (e.g. market and operational) are excluded from the analysis.
2. In credit risk assessment, there is no difference between debtors of different credit quality and rating.
3. Emphasis is on book values and not market values.
4. Inadequate assessment of risks and effects of the use of new financial instruments, as well as risk mitigation techniques.

Some of the weaknesses of Basel I, especially those related to market risk, were over-bridged by the amendment to recommendations from 1993 and 1996, by means of introducing capital requirements for market risk.

6.3 Basel II Norms

Linking of risks with capital in terms of the Basel I Accord needed a revision for these reasons:

1. Credit risk assessment under Basel I was not risk sensitive enough. It was not being able to differentiate between banks with lower risks and banks with higher risks.
2. It did not recognise the role of credit risk mitigation such as credit derivatives, securitization, collaterals and guarantees, in reducing risks.
3. It did not take into account operational risks of banks.
4. It promotes financial decision-making on the basis of regulatory constraints rather than on the basis of economic opportunities.

Thus, on June 26, 2004, The Basel Committee on Banking Supervision released "International Convergence of Capital Measurement and Capital Standards: A Revised Framework", which is commonly known as Basel II Accord. Basel I initially had credit risk and afterwards included market risk. In Basel II, apart from credit and market risk, *operational risk* was considered in capital adequacy ratio calculation. The focus of Basel II is on risk determination and quantification of credit, market and operational risks faced by banks. The fundamental objectives to revise the 1988 Accord were:

- To develop a framework that would strengthen the soundness and stability of the international banking system.
- To ensure that it does not become a source of competitive inequality among internationally active banks and yet have a capital adequacy regulation that is sufficiently consistent.
- To help promote the adoption of stronger risk management practices by the banking industry.

The RBI has accepted the Accord and issued guidelines to ensure compliance with the norms. It is a comprehensive framework of banking supervision. It insists on setting up rigorous risk and capital management requirements designed to ensure that a bank holds capital reserves appropriate to the risk. The underlying assumption here is that greater the risk to which a bank is exposed, greater the amount of capital it needs to hold to safeguard its solvency and overall economic stability. It also obliges banks to enhance disclosures.

Basel II provides spectrum of approaches for the measurement of credit, market and operational risks to determine the capital required. The spread and nature of the ownership structure is important as it impinges on the propensity to induct additional capital. While getting support from a large body of shareholders is a difficult proposition when the bank's performance is adverse, a smaller shareholder base constrains the ability of the bank to garner funds. Tier-I capital is not owed to anyone and is available to cover possible unexpected losses.

It has no maturity or repayment requirement, and is expected to remain a permanent component of the core capital of the counter party. While Basel standards currently require banks to have a capital adequacy ratio of 8 percent with Tier-I not less than 4 percent, RBI has mandated the banks to maintain a CAR of 9 percent. The maintenance of capital adequacy is like aiming at a moving target as the composition of risk-weighted assets gets changed every minute on account of fluctuation in the risk profile of a bank. Tier-I capital is known as the core capital, providing permanent and readily available support to the bank to meet the unexpected losses. The Basel II Accord focuses on three aspects:

1. Minimum capital requirement.
2. Supervisory review by Central Bank to monitor bank's capital adequacy and internal assessment process.
3. Market discipline by effective disclosure to encourage safe and sound banking practices.

6.3.1 Structure of Basel II: Basel II is designed to improve the way regulatory capital reflects the underlying risk. It consists of three 'pillars' which enshrine the key principles of the new regime. Collectively, they go well beyond the mechanistic calculation of minimum capital levels set by Basel I, allowing lenders to use their own models to calculate regulatory capital while seeking to ensure that they establish a culture, with risk management at the heart of the organization up to the highest managerial level. The efficient functioning of markets requires participants to have confidence in each other's stability and ability to transact business.

Capital rules foster this confidence because they require each member of the financial community to have, among other things, adequate capital to protect a financial organisation's depositors and counterparties from the risks of the institution's *on- and off-balance sheet risks.* At the top of the list are credit and market risks and not surprisingly, banks are required to set aside capital to cover these two main risks. Capital standards should be designed to allow a firm to absorb its losses, and in the worst case, to allow a firm to wind up its business without loss to customers, counterparties and without disrupting the orderly functioning of financial markets.

6.3.2 Capital: Tiers-1 and 2:

A. Tier-1 capital (core capital) is the most reliable form of capital. The major components are paid-up equity share capital and disclosed reserves, viz. statutory reserves, general reserves, capital reserves (other than revaluation reserves) and any other type of instrument notified by the RBI for inclusion. Examples of Tier-1 capital are common stock, preferred stock that is irredeemable and non-cumulative and retained earnings.

B. Tier-2 capital (supplementary capital) is a measure of a bank's financial strength with regard to the second most reliable form of financial capital. It consists mainly of undisclosed reserves, revaluation reserves, general provisions, subordinated debt and hybrid instruments.

This capital is less permanent in nature. The former absorbs losses without the bank being required to cease functioning, while the latter absorbs losses in the event of winding-up and thus provides a lesser degree of protection to depositors.

6.3.3 Conceptual Framework of Basel II Norms: This specifies that liquidity and solvency should be covered by a standard that provides for a bank to have sufficient liquid assets to meet its obligations given the risks it faces. It is also designed to improve the way regulatory capital reflects the underlying risk. Under Basel I, CAR includes credit risk, with market risk added later. While under Basel II, CAR consists of operational risk besides credit and market risks, it should be noted that RBI has suggested CAR of 9 percent while it is set at 8 percent internationally. The banks in India have kept a CAR in excess of 9 percent depending on the riskiness of assets in their portfolio. Basel II norms consist of three pillars.

The first pillar, *minimum capital requirements,* develops and expands on the standardised 1988 rules. The risk weighting system describes and replaces the earlier system by using external credit ratings. The second pillar is the *supervisory review of capital adequacy* which seeks to ensure that a bank's position is consistent with its overall risk profile and strategy, and as such encourages early supervisory intervention. Supervisors want the ability to require banks which show a greater degree of risk to hold a minimum capital in excess of 8 percent. The third pillar, *market discipline,* encourages high disclosure standards and enhances the role of market participants in encouraging banks to hold adequate capital.

A. Pillar 1: Minimum Regulatory Capital

Pillar 1 spells out the capital requirement of a bank in relation to the credit risk in its portfolio, which is a significant change from the "one-size fits all" approach of Basel I. Its primary objectives are to increase the risk sensitivity of capital requirements and align them more closely to the core risks that banks face. These risks include:

- **Credit risk**, which refers to the risk of loss arising from a borrower defaulting on their obligations;
- **Operational risk**, which is the risk of loss resulting from inadequate or failed internal processes, people, and systems, or from external events;
- **Traded market risk**, which refers to the risk of loss from holding financial instruments for trading purposes and arises due to movements in market prices, such as interest

rates, exchange rates, and equity values; and

- **Securitization risk**, which refers to the risk of loss associated with buying or selling asset-backed securities.

Pillar 1 allows flexibility to banks and supervisors to choose from among the standardised approach, internal ratings based approach, and securitisation framework methods to calculate the capital requirement for credit risk exposures. Besides, Pillar 1 sets out the allocation of capital for operational risk and market risk in the trading books of banks.

B. Pillar 2: Supervisory Review: Pillar 2 is meant to identify the risk factors not captured in Pillar 1, giving regulators discretion to adjust the regulatory capital requirement against that calculated under Pillar 1. For most lenders, the Pillar 2 process results in a higher regulatory capital requirement. Pillar 2 requires banks to think about the whole spectrum of risks they might face including those not captured at all in Pillar 1 such as the interest rate risk.

C. Pillar 3: Market Discipline: Pillar 3 is designed to increase the transparency of the lenders' risk profile by requiring them to give details of their risk management and risk distribution system. Information is released through the normal mandatory financial statements that lenders are required to publish or through lenders' websites.

6.3.4 Implications of Basel II Norms: The impact of these norms on the banking sector has been a topic on which a lot has been said and done and it is quite interesting. There will be an increased emphasis on risk management, the supervisory review process and market discipline.

The three pillars of Basel II are to support the Indian banking system so that the standards match the international standards. Banks in India observe CAR in line with the recommendations of the Basel committee. Prior to this, CAR was very low *being at* just 1.5 percent of the risk-weighted assets. There has been a considerable amount of debate concerning the potential implications of Basel II. Perhaps the most obvious effect is the change in the return on regulatory capital by altering the denominator. For residential mortgages, the release of regulatory capital under both the standardized and retail IRB approaches should be considerable. Many commentators see this as the basis for significant changes in industry pricing once the Basel I capital floors are removed and lenders move entirely to Basel II as the determinant of regulatory capital, which they believe could alter the competitive landscape and drive consolidation. It is pertinent to note a few key implications of Basel II norms in the Indian banking scenario.

A. Requirement of Additional Capital: Banks in India are adhering to a higher CAR than stipulated minimum, in order to have a better cushion to absorb possible shocks. Otherwise, they may face problems in view of the present competition and risk factors.

It is feared that some of the banks may not be able to infuse additional capital to comply with the new regulations and may thus be isolated from the global banking system.

B. Increased level of NPA: Though it is claimed that NPA level of banks has come down, the ground reality is that it still remains high. A large number of Indian banks have a significant proportion of NPA in their assets due to the poor quality of loans. Hence, there is a danger that banks may not be in a position to survive in the new environment as they will be unable to restructure themselves. Therefore, they may be forced to merge with other banks which would mean loss of capital to the banking system.

C. Costly database creation: Improved risk management and measurement are the needs of Basel II which aims at giving an impetus to the internal rating system of banks. One of the biggest challenges that Indian banks face is the high cost of database creation as detailed data is required, covering at least five years. This is tedious. Banks have to use an internally developed model whose impact may not be certain.

D. Low Degree of Corporate Rating Penetration: India has as few as five established rating agencies and the level of rating penetration is not very significant as, so far, ratings are restricted to issues and issuers. While Basel II gives some scope to extend the rating of issues to issuers, this would only be an approximation and it would be necessary for the system to move to ratings of issuers which poses a challenge.

E. Cross Border Issues for Foreign Banks: In India, foreign banks are statutorily required to maintain local capital and hence the following issues are required to be resolved: validation of the internal models approved by their head offices and home country supervisor adopted by the Indian branches of foreign banks.

6.4 Basel III Accord

Basel III guidelines were released in December 2010. Basel III is the global regulatory standard (agreed upon by the members of the Basel Committee on Banking Supervision) on bank capital adequacy, stress testing and market liquidity risk. (Basel I and Basel II are the earlier versions of the same, and were less stringent).

The financial crisis of 2008 was the main reason behind the introduction of these norms. A need was felt to further strengthen the system as banks in the developed economies were under-capitalised, over-leveraged and had a greater reliance on short-term funding. Also, the quantity and quality of capital under Basel II were deemed insufficient to contain any further risk.

These norms aim at making most banking activities such as their trading book activities, more capital intensive. The purpose is to promote a more resilient banking system by focusing on four vital banking parameters viz. capital, leverage, funding and liquidity.

According to Basel Committee on Banking Supervision, "Basel III is a comprehensive set of reform measures, developed by the Basel Committee on Banking Supervision, to strengthen the regulation, supervision and risk management of the banking sector".

Thus, we can say that Basel III is only a continuation of effort initiated by the Basel Committee on Banking Supervision to enhance the banking regulatory framework under Basel I and Basel II. This latest Accord now seeks to improve the banking sector's ability to deal with financial and economic stress, improve risk management and strengthen the banks' transparency.

6.4.1 Objectives of Basel III: Basel III measures aim to:

- Improve the banking sector's ability to absorb shocks arising from financial and economic stress, whatever the source.
- Improve risk management and governance.
- Strengthen banks' transparency and disclosures.

Thus, Basel III guidelines are aimed at to improve the ability of banks to withstand periods of economic and financial stress as the new guidelines are more stringent than the earlier requirements for capital and liquidity in the banking sector.

6.4.2 Basel III Requirements and Indian Banks: The Basel III which is to be implemented by banks in India as per the guidelines issued by RBI from time to time will be a challenging task not only for the banks but also for Government. It is estimated that Indian banks will be required to raise ₹ 6,00,000 crore in external capital by 2020 (the estimates vary from organisation to organization). Expansion of capital to this extent will affect the returns on the equity of these banks especially public sector banks. However, only consolation for Indian banks is the fact that historically they have maintained their core and overall capital well in excess of the regulatory minimum.

6.4.3 Three Pillars of Basel III Norms: Anyone who has ever heard about Basel I and II, most likely must have heard about Three Pillars of Basel. Three Pillars of Basel still stand under Basel III.

Basel III has essentially been designed to address the weaknesses that become too obvious during the 2008 financial crisis world faced. The intent of the Basel Committee seems to prepare the banking industry for any future economic downturns. The framework enhances bank-specific measures and includes macro-prudential regulations to help create a more stable banking sector.

The basic structure of Basel III remains unchanged with three mutually reinforcing pillars.

Pillar 1: Minimum regulatory capital requirements based on risk weighted assets (RWAs): Maintaining capital calculated through credit, market and operational risk areas.

Pillar 2: Supervisory review process: Regulating tools and frameworks for dealing with peripheral risks that banks face.

Pillar 3: Market Discipline: Increasing the disclosures that banks must provide to increase the transparency of banks.

6.4.4 Major Features of Basel III

A. Better Capital Quality: One of the key elements of Basel III is the introduction of much stricter definition of capital. Better quality capital means the higher loss-absorbing capacity. This in turn will mean that banks will be stronger, allowing them to better withstand periods of stress. Banks will be required to hold more reserves by January 1, 2015, with common equity requirements raised to 4.5 percent from 2 percent. Tier-1 capital requirements: Under the new rules, the mandatory reserve (known as Tier-1 capital) will be raised from 4 percent to 6 percent by 2015. Banks in India are required to maintain a minimum Pillar 1 capital to risk weighted assets ratio (CRAR) of 9 percent on an ongoing basis (other than capital conservation buffer and countercyclical capital buffer). With a view to improving the quality and quantity of regulatory capital, it has been decided that the predominant form of Tier-1 capital must be common equity; since it is critical that banks' risk exposures are backed by high quality capital base. Non-equity Tier-1 and Tier-2 capital would continue to form part of the regulatory capital subject to eligibility criteria as laid down in Basel III.

B. Capital Conservation Buffer: Another key feature of Basel III is that now banks will be required to hold a capital conservation buffer of 2.5 percent. This buffer was introduced to meet one of the four key objectives identified by the Committee in the December 2009 consultative document, "*Strengthening the Resilience of the Banking Sector*", which stated, "conserve enough capital to build buffers at individual banks and the entire banking sector which can then be used in times of stress. If a bank has complied with the minimum common equity Tier-1 and Tier-1 capital ratios, then the excess additional Tier-1 capital can be admitted for compliance with the minimum CRAR of 9 percent of RWAs. In addition to the minimum common equity Tier-1 capital of 5.5 percent of RWAs, banks are also required to maintain a capital conservation buffer (CCB) of 2.5 percent of RWAs in the form of common equity Tier-1 capital. The aim of asking to build conservation buffer is to ensure that banks maintain a cushion of capital that can be used to absorb losses during periods of financial and economic stress.

C. Countercyclical Buffer: This is also one of the key elements of Basel III. The countercyclical buffer has been introduced with the objective to increase capital requirements in good times and decrease the same in bad times. The buffer will slow banking activity when it overheats and will encourage lending when times are tough i.e. in bad times. The buffer will range from 0 percent to 2.5 percent, consisting of common equity or other fully loss-absorbing capital.

D. Minimum Common Equity and Tier-1 Capital Requirements: The minimum requirement for common equity, the highest form of loss-absorbing capital, has been raised under Basel III from 2 percent to 4.5 percent of total risk-weighted assets. The overall Tier-1 capital requirement, consisting of not only common equity but also other qualifying financial instruments, will also increase from the current minimum of 4 percent to 6 percent. Although the minimum total capital requirement will remain at the current 8 percent level, yet the required total capital will increase to 10.5 percent when combined with the conservation buffer.

E. Leverage Ratio (Ratio of Tier-I Capital to Total Assets): A review of the financial crisis of 2008 has indicted that the value of many assets fell quicker than assumed from historical experience. Thus, now Basel III rules include a leverage ratio to serve as a safety net. A leverage ratio is the relative amount of capital to total assets (not risk-weighted). This aims to put a cap on swelling of leverage in the banking sector on a global basis. 3 percent leverage ratio of Tier-1 will be tested before a mandatory leverage ratio is introduced in January 2018.

F. Liquidity Ratios: Under Basel III, a framework for liquidity risk management will be created—a new liquidity coverage ratio (LCR). It is designed to ensure that a bank maintains an adequate level of unencumbered, high-quality assets that can be converted into cash to meet its liquidity needs for a 30-day time horizon under an acute liquidity stress scenario specified by supervisors. The standard requires that the ratio be no lower than 100 percent. Its implementation is planned for 2015. To ensure that investment banking inventories, off-balance sheet exposures, securitization pipelines and other assets and activities are funded with at least a minimum amount of stable liabilities in relation to their liquidity risk profiles, the new Accord introduces net funding stability ratio (NFSR). It is defined as the ratio, for a bank, of its "available amount of stable funding" divided by its "required amount of stable funding". The standard requires that the ratio be no lower than 100 percent.

G. Systemically Important Financial Institutions (SIFI): As part of the macro-prudential framework, systemically important banks will be expected to have loss-absorbing capability beyond the Basel III requirements. Options for implementation include capital surcharges, contingent capital and bail-in-debt.

6.5 How is Basel III an Improvement over Basel II?

Thus, the enhancements of Basel III over Basel II come primarily in four areas: (i) augmentation in the level and quality of capital; (ii) introduction of liquidity standards; (iii) modifications in provisioning norms; and (iv) better and more comprehensive disclosures.

6.5.1 Higher Capital Requirement: Basel III requires higher and better quality capital. The minimum total capital remains unchanged at 8 percent of risk weighted assets (RWA). However, Basel III introduces a capital conservation buffer of 2.5 percent of RWA over and above the minimum capital requirement, raising the total capital requirement to 10.5 percent against the 8 percent under Basel II. This buffer is intended to ensure that banks are able to absorb losses without breaching the minimum capital requirement, and are able to carry on business even in a downturn without deleveraging. This buffer is not part of the regulatory minimum; however, the level of the buffer will determine the dividend distributed to shareholders and the bonus paid to staff.

6.5.2 Liquidity Standards: To mitigate liquidity risk, Basel III addresses both potential short-term liquidity stress and long-term structural liquidity mismatches in banks' balance sheets. To cover short-term liquidity stress, banks will be required to maintain sufficient high-quality unencumbered liquid assets to withstand any stressed funding scenario over a 30-day horizon as measured by the liquidity coverage ratio (LCR). To mitigate liquidity mismatches in the long-term, banks will be mandated to maintain a net stable funding ratio (NSFR). The NSFR mandates a minimum amount of stable sources of funding relative to the liquidity profile of the assets, as well as the potential for contingent liquidity needs arising from off-balance sheet commitments over a one year horizon. In essence, the NSFR is aimed at encouraging banks to exploit stable sources of funding.

6.5.3 Provisioning Norms: The Basel Committee is

supporting the proposal for adoption of an 'expected loss' based measure of provisioning which captures actual losses more transparently and is also less pro-cyclical than the current 'incurred loss' approach. The expected loss approach for provisioning will make financial reporting more useful for all stakeholders, including regulators and supervisors.

6.5.4 Disclosure Requirement: The disclosures made by banks are important for market participants to make informed decisions. One of the lessons of the crisis is that the disclosures made by banks in their risky exposures and on regulatory capital were neither appropriate nor sufficiently transparent to afford any comparative analysis. To remedy this, Basel III requires banks to disclose all relevant details, including any regulatory adjustments, as regards the composition of the regulatory capital of the bank.

7

Liquidity Risk Management

7.1 Liquidity Defined

Bank management is the process in which banking resources are properly utilized for achieving the banking objectives. In order to achieve the desired objectives, a bank manager has to consider the four basic concerns such as:

Liquidity management=Making sure that the bank has enough cash to cover depositors' requests for withdrawals (deposit outflows).

Asset management = Acquiring assets with the highest return and the lowest risk.

Liability management=Acquiring funds at the lowest cost.

Capital adequacy management=Maintaining sufficient capital while still providing decent returns to shareholders.

Liquidity, which is represented by the quality and marketability of assets and liabilities expose the organisation to liquidity risks. Unlike other risks like market risk, interest rate risk, operational and technology risks and foreign exchange risks that can threaten the solvency of a bank, liquidity risk is a normal aspect of everyday management of a financial institution. Only in extreme cases do liquidity risk problems translate into solvency risk problems. Banks need liquidity to meet deposit withdrawals and to fund loan demands.

Traditionally, liquidity has been defined as the capacity of financial institutions to finance increases in their assets and comply with their liabilities as these mature. Bank liquidity has two distinct but interrelated dimensions: liability (or cash) liquidity, which refers to the ability to obtain funding on the market and asset (or market) liquidity, associated with the possibility of selling the assets. Both concepts are interrelated, and the interaction between them tends towards their mutual reinforcement.

Professor Sayers has described liquidity as, "the word that the banker uses to describe the ability to satisfy demands for cash in exchange of deposits".

Liquidity is the ability to efficiently accommodate deposit as also reduction in liabilities and to fund the loan growth and possible funding of the off-balance sheet claims. Liquidity is a bank's capacity to fund increase in assets and meet both expected and unexpected cash and collateral obligations at reasonable cost and without incurring unacceptable losses. Liquidity risk is the inability of a bank to meet such obligations as they become due, without adversely affecting the bank's financial condition. Liquidity risk is considered a major risk for banks. It arises when the cushion provided by the liquid assets are not sufficient enough to meet its obligation. In such a situation, banks often meet their liquidity requirements from market. However, conditions of funding through market depend upon liquidity in the market and borrowing institution's liquidity. Accordingly, an institution short of liquidity may have to undertake transaction at heavy cost resulting in a loss of earning or in worst case scenario the liquidity risk could result in bankruptcy of the institution if it is unable to undertake transaction even at current market prices.

Liquidity risk is the potential for loss to an institution arising from either its inability to meet its obligations or to fund increases in assets as they fall due without incurring unacceptable cost or losses. Banks with large off-balance sheet exposures or the banks, which rely heavily on large corporate deposits, have relatively high level of liquidity risk. Further, banks experiencing a rapid growth in assets should have major concern for liquidity. Liquidity risk may not be seen in isolation, because financial risk are not mutually exclusive and liquidity risk is often triggered by consequence of these other financial risks such as credit risk, market risk etc.

7.2 Liquidity Management: Conceptual Framework

The world of cash and liquidity management was once a simpler place. Access to capital was rarely a bottleneck, even for highly leveraged corporates, and many had strong, long standing relationships with a single bank that helped meet most of their funding and cash management needs. All of that changed with the global financial crisis of 2008-2009. Corporates around the world suddenly faced the backlash of the solvency of banks, the impact on their businesses if a banking provider collapsed, and the reigning in of lending to businesses by banks. These new challenges triggered a radical reshaping of the corporate treasury landscape and the way that corporates interacted with banks.

Cash and liquidity management are core elements of a successful treasury management operation and fundamental to maintaining a strong balance sheet. Appropriate liquidity management should ensure that we have enough cash available to meet all payment needs expected or unexpected. It involves forecasting, risk management, bank relationships, transparency and communication. Cash must be in the right place at the right time.

An optimal liquidity management framework should address the actual and potential cash needs; safety, diversification and accessibility of cash and short-term investments; and alternative and contingent funding sources. Liquidity management measures the ability of financial intermediary to meet demand for deposits, withdrawal and other cash outflows. Bank liquidity management policies should comprise a risk management structure, a liquidity management and funding strategy, a set of limits to liquidity risk exposures, and a set of procedures for liquidity planning under alternative scenarios, including crisis situations. Liquidity is necessary for banks to compensate for expected and unexpected balance sheet fluctuations and to provide funds for growth.

A bank has adequate liquidity potential when it can obtain needed funds promptly and at a reasonable cost. The price of liquidity is a function of market conditions and the market's perception of the inherent riskiness of the borrowing institution. Bank's liquidity management is the process of generating funds to meet contractual or relationship obligations at reasonable prices at all times. New loan demand, existing loan commitments, and deposit withdrawals are the basic contractual or relationship obligations that bank must meet. Effective liquidity management by bank serves five important functions:

- It demonstrates the market place that the bank is safe and therefore capable of repaying its borrowings.
- It enables bank to meet its prior loan commitments, whether formal or informal.
- It enables the bank to avoid unprofitable sale of assets. This function permits the banks to avoid sale of assets at fire sale prices, as opposed to going concern values to generate funds.
- It lowers the size of the default risk premium the bank must pay for funds. This function focuses on the reasonable price aspects of the definition of liquidity management. Banks with strong balance sheets will be perceived by the market place as being liquid and safe. Such banks will be able to buy funds at risk premium, reflecting their perceived creditworthiness.

7.3 Need for Liquidity Management

The fundamental role of banks in the maturity transformation of short-term deposits into long-term loans makes banks inherently vulnerable to liquidity risk, both of an institution-specific nature and that which affects markets as a whole. Liquidity management and its associated risks assume paramount importance under the overall asset liability management strategies. Liquidity risk management in banks is defined as the risk of being unable either to meet their obligations to depositors or to fund increases in assets as they fall due without incurring unacceptable costs or losses. This risk occurs when the depositors collectively decide to withdraw more funds than the bank immediately has on hand, or when the borrowers fail to meet their financial obligation to the banks.

In other words, liquidity risk occurs in two cases. Firstly, it arises symmetrically to the borrowers in their relationship with the banks, for example when the banks decide to terminate the loans but the borrowers cannot afford it. Secondly, it arises in the context of the banks' relationships with their depositors, for example, when the depositors decide to redeem their deposits but the banks cannot afford it. Liquidity risk management is of paramount importance because a liquidity shortfall at a single institution can have system-wide repercussions. Financial market developments in the past decade have increased the complexity of liquidity risk and its management.

The need for liquidity management arises from central banks' concept of liquidity, measured in terms of the monetary base, of which it is the monopoly supplier. The supply of monetary base by the central bank depends on: (i) the public's demand for currency, as determined by the size of monetary transactions and the opportunity cost of holding the money and, (ii) the banking system's need for reserves to settle or discharge payment obligations. In fulfilling these needs, central banks also attempt to control and modulate liquidity conditions by varying the supply of bank reserves to meet its macroeconomic objectives subject to the constraint of financial stability.

Bank reserves are, therefore, influenced through reserve requirements or open market operations. In so doing, central banks attempt to affect the level of short-term interest rates in a manner in which market movements of these interest rate movements are smoothened out as volatility of any monetary or non-monetary asset prices can be costly in terms of real output and investment decisions. It is from this standpoint that a central bank decides to modulate its market operations over a chosen time horizon to reflect its policy stance. Liquidity management of a central bank means supplying to the market the amount of liquidity that is consistent with a desired level of short-term interest rate. It is defined "as the framework, set of instruments and the rules that the central bank follows in order to manage the amount of money supply to control short-term interest rates with the objective of price stability".

7.4 Early Warning Indicators of Liquidity Risk

An incipient liquidity problem may initially reveal in the bank's financial monitoring system as a downward trend with potential long-term consequences for earnings or capital. Given below are some early warning indicators that not necessarily always lead to liquidity problem for a bank; however these have potential to ignite such a problem. Consequently, management needs to watch carefully such indicators and exercise further scrutiny/analysis wherever it deems appropriate. Examples of such internal indicators are:

1. A negative trend or significantly increased risk in any area or product line.
2. Concentrations in either assets or liabilities.
3. Deterioration in quality of credit portfolio.
4. A decline in earnings performance or projections.
5. Rapid asset growth funded by volatile large deposit.
6. A large size of off-balance sheet exposure.
7. Deteriorating third party evaluation about the bank.

A liquidity risk management involves not only analyzing banks' on- and off-balance sheet positions to forecast future cash flows but also how the funding requirement would be met. The latter involves identifying the funding market the bank has access to, understanding the nature of those markets, evaluating banks current and future use of the market and monitor signs of confidence erosion. Effective liquidity risk management helps ensure a bank's ability to meet its obligations as they fall due and reduces the probability of an adverse situation developing. This assumes significance on account of the fact that liquidity crisis, even at a single institution, can have systemic implications. Liquidity risk for banks are mainly of the following types:

- **Funding Risk:** The risk that a bank will not be able to meet efficiently the expected and unexpected current and future cash flows and collateral needs without affecting either its daily operations or its financial condition. Funding risk arises due to fraud, causing substantial loss; systematic risk; loss of confidence; liabilities in foreign currencies.
- **Time Risk:** Need to compensate for non-receipt of expected inflows of funds, arises due to severe deterioration in the asset quality; standard assets turning into non-performing assets; time involved in managing liquidity; temporary problems in recovery.
- **Call Risk:** Crystallization of contingent liabilities and inability to undertake profitable business opportunities when desirable, arise due to swaps and options; conversion of non-fund based limit into fund based.

Adequacy of a bank's liquidity position depends upon an analysis of the following factors:

- Historical funding requirements.
- Current liquidity position.
- Sources of funds.
- Anticipated future funding needs.
- Options for reducing funding needs.
- Present and anticipated asset quality.
- Present and future earnings capacity.
- Present and planned capital position.

The liquidity position of a bank is affected by the factors like a decline in earnings, an increase in NPAs, deposit concentrations, expanded business opportunities, acquisitions, new tax initiatives and downgrading by rating agencies.

7.5 Governance of Liquidity Risk Management

The Reserve Bank had issued guidelines on asset liability management (ALM) system, covering *inter alia* liquidity risk management system, in February 1999 and October 2007. Successful implementation of any risk management process has to emanate from the top management in the bank with the demonstration of its strong commitment to integrate basic operations and strategic decision-making with risk management. Ideally, the organisational set up for liquidity risk management should be as under:

- Board of directors (BoD).
- Risk management committee.
- Asset-liability management committee (ALCO).
- Asset liability management (ALM) support group.

BoD should have the overall responsibility for management of liquidity risk. The board should decide the strategy, policies and procedures of the bank to manage liquidity risk in accordance with the liquidity risk tolerance/limits.

The risk tolerance should be clearly understood at all levels of management. The board should also ensure that it understands the nature of the liquidity risk of the bank including liquidity risk profile of all branches, subsidiaries and associates (both domestic and overseas), periodically reviews information necessary to maintain this understanding, establishes executive-level lines of authority and responsibility for managing the bank's liquidity risk, enforces management's duties to identify, measure, monitor, and manage liquidity risk and formulates/reviews the contingent funding plan.

Risk management committee, which reports to the board, consisting of chief executive officer (CEO)/chairman and managing director (CMD) and heads of credit, market and operational risk management committee should be responsible for evaluating the overall risks faced by the bank including liquidity risk. The potential interaction of liquidity risk with other risks should also be included in the risks addressed by the risk management committee.

Asset-liability management committee (ALCO) consisting of the bank's top management should be responsible for ensuring adherence to the risk tolerance/limits set by the board as well as implementing the liquidity risk management strategy of the bank in line with bank's decided risk management objectives and risk tolerance.

To ensure commitment of the top management and timely response to market dynamics, the CEO/CMD or the executive director (ED) should head the committee. The chiefs of investment, credit, resource management or planning, funds management/treasury (forex and domestic), international banking and economic research may be members of the committee. In addition, the head of the technology division should also be an invitee for building up of MIS and related computerization. Some banks may even have sub-committees and support groups. The size (number of members) of ALCO would depend on the size of each institution, business mix and organizational complexity.

The role of the ALCO with respect to the liquidity risk should include, *inter alia*, the following:

1. Deciding on desired maturity profile and mix of incremental assets and liabilities.
2. Deciding on source and mix of liabilities or sale of assets. Towards this end, it will have to develop a view on future direction of interest rate movements and decide on funding mixes between fixed vs. floating rate funds, wholesale vs. retail deposits, money market vs. capital market funding, domestic vs. foreign currency funding, etc. ALCO should be aware of the composition, characteristics and diversification of the bank's assets and funding sources and should regularly review the funding strategy in the light of any changes in the internal or external environments.
3. Determining the structure, responsibilities and controls for managing liquidity risk and for overseeing the liquidity positions of all branches and legal entities like subsidiaries, joint ventures and associates in which a bank is active, and outline these elements clearly in the bank's liquidity policy.
4. Ensuring operational independence of liquidity risk management function, with adequate support of skilled and experienced officers.
5. Ensuring adequacy of cash flow projections and the assumptions used.

6. Reviewing the stress test scenarios including the assumptions as well as the results of the stress tests and ensuring that a well-documented contingency funding plan is in place which is reviewed periodically.
7. Deciding the transfer pricing policy of the bank and making liquidity costs and benefits an integral part of bank's strategic planning.
8. Regularly reporting to the BoD and risk management committee on the liquidity risk profile of the bank.

ALCO should have a thorough understanding of the close links between funding liquidity risk and market liquidity risk, as well as how other risks including credit, market, operational and reputational risks affect the bank's overall liquidity risk strategy. Liquidity risk can often arise from perceived or actual weaknesses, failures or problems in the management of other risk types. It should, therefore, identify events that could have an impact on market and public perceptions about its soundness and reputation.

The ALM support group consisting of operating staff should be responsible for analysing, monitoring and reporting the liquidity risk profile to the ALCO. The group should also prepare forecasts (simulations) showing the effect of various possible changes in market conditions on the bank's liquidity position and recommend action needed to be taken to maintain the liquidity position/adhere to bank's internal limits.

The formality and sophistication of liquidity management depends on the size and sophistication of the bank, as well as the nature and complexity of its activities. Regardless of the bank, good management information systems, strong analysis of funding requirements under alternative scenarios, diversification of funding sources, and contingency planning are crucial elements of strong liquidity management.

7.6 Liquidity Principles

Following five key principles can help to manage a bank's liquidity more effectively:

1. Understand and categorize its cash needs, then determine an appropriate (not necessarily minimum) liquidity requirement.
2. Establish appropriate investment guidelines focusing on availability and safety.
3. Select investment types within guidelines that are appropriate for each cash category.
4. Establish and verify diversified contingent funding sources.
5. Maximize the transparency and efficiency of the cash position across geographies and legal entities.

In February 2008, the Basel Committee on Banking Supervision published 'Liquidity Risk Management and Supervisory Challenges'. The difficulties outlined in that paper highlighted that many banks had failed to take account of a number of basic principles of liquidity risk management when liquidity was plentiful. Many of the most exposed banks did not have an adequate framework that satisfactorily accounted for the liquidity risks posed by individual products and business lines, and therefore incentives at the business level were misaligned with the overall risk tolerance of the bank. Many banks had not considered the amount of liquidity they might need to satisfy contingent obligations, either contractual or non-contractual, as they viewed funding of these obligations to be highly unlikely.

In order to account for financial market developments as well as lessons learnt from the turmoil, the Basel Committee conducted a fundamental review of its '2000 Sound Practices for Managing Liquidity in Banking Organisations'. Guidance has been significantly expanded in a number of key areas. In particular, more detailed guidance is provided on:

1. The importance of establishing a liquidity risk tolerance.
2. The maintenance of an adequate level of liquidity, including through a cushion of liquid assets.
3. The necessity of allocating liquidity costs, benefits and risks to all significant business activities.

4. The identification and measurement of the full range of liquidity risks, including contingent liquidity risks.
5. The design and use of severe stress test scenarios.
6. The need for a robust and operational contingency funding plan.
7. The management of intra-day liquidity risk and collateral.
8. Public disclosure in promoting market discipline.

Guidance for supervisors also has been augmented substantially. Guidance emphasises the importance of supervisors assessing the adequacy of a bank's liquidity risk management framework and its level of liquidity, and suggests steps that supervisors should take if these are deemed inadequate.

The principles also stress the importance of effective cooperation between supervisors and other key stakeholders, such as central banks, especially in times of stress. This guidance focuses on liquidity risk management at medium and large complex banks, but the sound principles have broad applicability to all types of banks.

The implementation of the sound principles by both banks and supervisors should be tailored to the size, nature of business and complexity of a bank's activities. A bank and its supervisors should also consider the bank's role in the financial sectors of the jurisdictions in which it operates and the bank's systemic importance in those financial sectors. The Basel Committee fully expects banks and national supervisors to implement the revised principles promptly and thoroughly and the Committee will actively review progress in implementation. This guidance is arranged around seventeen principles for managing and supervising liquidity risk.

In practice, the banks regularly find imbalances (gaps) between the asset and the liability side that need to be equalized because, by nature, banks accept liquid liabilities but invest in illiquid. If a bank fails to balance such a gap, liquidity risk might occur, followed by some undesirable consequences such as insolvency risk, government bailout risk, and reputation risk. The failure or inefficiency of liquidity management is caused by the strength of liquidity pressure, the preparation of a bank's liquid instruments, the bank's condition at the time of liquidity pressure, and the inability of the bank to find internal or external liquid sources.

7.7 Basic Principles for the Management and Supervision of Liquidity Risk

7.7.1 General

Principle 1: A bank is responsible for the sound management of liquidity risk. A bank should establish a robust liquidity risk management framework that ensures it maintains sufficient liquidity, including a cushion of unencumbered, high quality liquid assets, to withstand a range of stress events, including those involving the loss or impairment of both unsecured and secured funding sources.

Supervisors should assess the adequacy of both a bank's liquidity risk management framework and its liquidity position and should take prompt action if a bank is deficient in either area in order to protect depositors and to limit potential damage to the financial system.

In RBI's overall management, short-term liquidity management occupies a very important place due to following factors:

1. In financial sector, in 1990s, many reforms were introduced. The important reforms are deregulation of interest rates and exchange rates. Earlier, these rates were determined by the RBI; after reforms, they are determined by demand and supply. RBI in absence of direct intervention indirectly influences these rates by using multiple indicators approach.
2. Due to liberalization, capital flows between countries have increased.
3. Foreign capital flows have increased employment. It adds to the supply of foreign exchange and has resulted into appreciation of domestic currency. With this, the exports

have become more expensive.

4. When capital inflows are converted into rupees, they get injected into the economy, thereby increasing the money supply.

Hence, to maintain the price stability, RBI has to manage the exchange rate and interest rate.

7.7.2 Governance of Liquidity Risk Management

Principle 2: A bank should clearly articulate a liquidity risk tolerance that is appropriate for its business strategy and its role in the financial system.

Principle 3: Senior management should develop strategies, policies and practices to manage liquidity risk in accordance with the risk tolerance and to ensure that the bank maintains sufficient liquidity. Senior management should continuously review information on the bank's liquidity developments and report to the board of directors on a regular basis. A bank's board of directors should review and approve the strategies, policies and practices related to the management of liquidity at least annually and ensure that senior management manages liquidity risk effectively.

Principle 4: A bank should incorporate liquidity costs, benefits and risks in the internal pricing, performance measurement and new product approval process for all significant business activities (both on- and off-balance sheet), thereby aligning the risk-taking incentives of individual business lines with the liquidity risk exposures their activities create for the bank as a whole.

7.7.3 Measurement and Management of Liquidity Risk:

Principle 5: A bank should have a sound process for identifying, measuring, monitoring and controlling liquidity risk. This process should include a robust framework for comprehensively projecting cash flows arising from assets, liabilities and off-balance sheet items over an appropriate set of time horizons.

Principle 6: A bank should actively monitor and control liquidity risk exposures and funding needs within and across legal entities, business lines and currencies, taking into account legal, regulatory and operational limitations to the transferability of liquidity.

Principle 7: A bank should establish a funding strategy that provides effective diversification in the sources and tenor of funding. It should maintain an ongoing presence in its chosen funding markets and strong relationships with funds providers to promote effective diversification of funding sources. A bank should regularly gauge its capacity to raise funds quickly from each source. It should identify the main factors that affect its ability to raise funds and monitor those factors closely to ensure that estimates of fund raising capacity remain valid.

Principle 8: A bank should actively manage its intraday liquidity positions and risks to meet payment and settlement obligations on a timely basis under both normal and stressed conditions and thus contribute to the smooth functioning of payment and settlement systems.

Principle 9: A bank should actively manage its collateral positions, differentiating between encumbered and unencumbered assets. A bank should monitor the legal entity and physical location where collateral is held and how it may be mobilized in a timely manner.

Principle 10: A bank should conduct stress tests on a regular basis for a variety of short-term and protracted institution-specific and market-wide stress scenarios (individually and in combination) to identify sources of potential liquidity strain and to ensure that current exposures remain in accordance with a bank's established liquidity risk tolerance. A bank should use stress test outcomes to adjust its liquidity risk management strategies, policies, and positions and to develop effective contingency plans.

Principle 11: A bank should have a formal contingency funding plan (CFP) that clearly sets out the strategies for addressing liquidity shortfalls in emergency situations. A CFP should outline policies to manage a range of stress environments, establish clear lines of responsibility, include clear invocation and escalation procedures and be regularly tested and updated to ensure that it is operationally robust.

Principle 12: A bank should maintain a cushion of unencumbered, high quality liquid assets to be held as insurance against a range of liquidity stress scenarios, including those that involve the loss or impairment of unsecured and typically available secured funding sources. There should be no legal, regulatory or operational impediment to using these assets to obtain funding.

7.7.4 Public Disclosure

Principle 13: A bank should publicly disclose information on a regular basis that enables market participants to make an informed judgement about the soundness of its liquidity risk management framework and liquidity position.

7.7.5 Role of Supervisors

Principle 14: Supervisors should regularly perform a comprehensive assessment of a bank's overall liquidity risk management framework and liquidity position to determine whether they deliver an adequate level of resilience to liquidity stress given the bank's role in the financial system.

Principle 15: Supervisors should supplement their regular assessments of a bank's liquidity risk management framework and liquidity position by monitoring a combination of internal reports, prudential reports and market information.

Principle 16: Supervisors should intervene to require effective and timely remedial action by a bank to address deficiencies in its liquidity risk management processes or liquidity position.

Principle 17: Supervisors should communicate with other supervisors and public authorities, such as central banks, both within and across national borders, to facilitate effective cooperation regarding the supervision and oversight of liquidity risk management. Communication should occur regularly during normal times, with the nature and frequency of the information sharing increasing as appropriate during times of stress.

7.8 Requirements of a Sound Liquidity Risk Management System

A sound liquidity risk management system should incorporate the following:

1. A bank should establish a robust liquidity risk management framework.
2. The board of directors (BoD) of a bank should be responsible for sound management of liquidity risk and should clearly articulate a liquidity risk tolerance appropriate for its business strategy and its role in the financial system.
3. The BoD should develop strategy, policies and practices to manage liquidity risk in accordance with the risk tolerance and ensure that the bank maintains sufficient liquidity. The BoD should review the strategy, policies and practices at least annually.
4. Top management/ALCO should continuously review information on bank's liquidity developments and report to the BoD on a regular basis.
5. A bank should have a sound process for identifying, measuring, monitoring and controlling liquidity risk, including a robust framework for comprehensively projecting cash flows arising from assets, liabilities and off-balance sheet items over an appropriate time horizon.
6. A bank's liquidity management process should be sufficient to meet its funding needs and cover both expected and unexpected deviations from normal operations.
7. A bank should incorporate liquidity costs, benefits and risks in internal pricing, performance measurement and new product approval process for all significant business activities.
8. A bank should actively monitor and manage liquidity risk exposure and funding needs within and across legal entities, business lines and currencies, taking into account legal, regulatory and operational limitations to transferability of liquidity.

   A bank should establish a funding strategy that provides

effective diversification in the source and tenor of funding, and maintain ongoing presence in its chosen funding markets and counterparties, and address inhibiting factors in this regard.

1. Senior management should ensure that market access is being actively managed, monitored, and tested by the appropriate staff.
2. A bank should identify alternate sources of funding that strengthen its capacity to withstand a variety of severe bank specific and market-wide liquidity shocks.
3. A bank should actively manage its intra-day liquidity positions and risks.
4. A bank should actively manage its collateral positions.
5. A bank should conduct stress tests on a regular basis for short-term and protracted institution-specific and market-wide stress scenarios and use stress test outcomes to adjust its liquidity risk management strategies, policies and position and develop effective contingency plans.
6. Senior management of banks should monitor for potential liquidity stress events by using early warning indicators and event triggers. Early warning signals may include, but are not limited to, negative publicity concerning an asset class owned by the bank, increased potential for deterioration in the bank's financial condition, widening debt or credit default swap spreads, and increased concerns over the funding of off-balance sheet items.
7. To mitigate the potential for reputation contagion, a bank should have a system of effective communication with counterparties, credit rating agencies, and other stakeholders when liquidity problems arise.
8. A bank should have a formal contingency funding plan (CFP) that clearly sets out the strategies for addressing liquidity shortfalls in emergency situations. A CFP should delineate policies to manage a range of stress environments, establish clear lines of responsibility, and articulate clear implementation and escalation procedures.
9. A bank should maintain a cushion of unencumbered, high

quality liquid assets to be held as insurance against a range of liquidity stress scenarios.

10. A bank should publicly disclose its liquidity information on a regular basis that enables market participants to make an informed judgment about the soundness of its liquidity risk management framework and liquidity position.

7.9 Measuring and Managing Liquidity Risk

The most important activity of commercial banks is to measure and manage liquidity risk. Following steps are necessary for managing liquidity risks in banks:

- Developing a structure for managing liquidity risk;
- Setting tolerance level and limit for liquidity risk; and
- Measuring and managing liquidity risk.

Sound liquidity risk management involves a strategy for the bank, ensuring effective board and senior management oversight as well as operating under a sound process for measuring, monitoring and controlling liquidity risk. A bank should define and identify the liquidity risk to which it is exposed for all legal entities, branches and subsidiaries in the jurisdictions in which it is active. A bank's liquidity needs and the sources of liquidity available to meet those needs depend significantly on the bank's business and product mix, balance sheet structure and cash flow profiles of its on- and off-balance sheet obligations. As a result, a bank should evaluate each major on- and off-balance sheet position, including the effect of embedded options and other contingent exposures that may affect the bank's sources and uses of funds, and determine how it can affect liquidity risk.

A bank should consider the interactions between exposures to funding liquidity risk and market liquidity risk. A bank that obtains liquidity from capital markets should recognise that these sources may be more volatile than traditional retail deposits. A bank should actively monitor and control liquidity risks at the level of individual legal entities, and foreign branches and subsidiaries, and the group as a whole, incorporating processes that aggregate data across multiple systems in order to develop a group-wide view of liquidity risk exposures and identify constraints on the transfer of liquidity within the group. For each country in which it is active, a bank should ensure that it has the necessary expertise about country-specific features of the legal and regulatory regime that influence liquidity risk management, including arrangements for dealing with failed banks, deposit insurance, and central bank operational frameworks and collateral policies. This knowledge should be reflected in liquidity risk management processes.

A bank should set a liquidity risk tolerance in light of its business objectives, strategic direction and overall risk appetite. The board of directors is ultimately responsible for the liquidity risk assumed by the bank and the manner in which this risk is managed and therefore should establish the bank's liquidity risk tolerance. The tolerance, which should define the level of liquidity risk that the bank is willing to assume, should be appropriate for the business strategy of the bank and its role in the financial system and should reflect the bank's financial condition and funding capacity. The tolerance should ensure that the firm manages its liquidity strongly in normal times in such a way that it is able to withstand a prolonged period of stress. The risk tolerance should be articulated in such a way that all levels of management clearly understand the trade-off between risks and profits. Senior management should develop strategies, policies and practices to manage liquidity risk in accordance with the risk tolerance and to ensure that the bank maintains sufficient liquidity.

Stress testing should form an integral part of the overall governance and liquidity risk management culture in banks. A stress test is commonly described as an evaluation of the financial position of a bank under a severe but plausible scenario to assist in decision-making within the bank. Stress testing alerts bank's management to adverse unexpected outcomes as it provides forward looking assessment of risk and facilitates better planning to address the vulnerabilities identified. The Reserve Bank had issued guidelines to banks on stress testing in June 2007, which requires banks to have in place a board approved "stress testing framework". Banks should ensure that the framework as detailed in the guidelines and as specified is put in place.

A bank should conduct stress tests on a regular basis for a variety of short-term and protracted bank specific and market wide stress scenarios (individually and in combination). In designing liquidity stress scenarios, the nature of the bank's business activities and vulnerabilities should be taken into consideration so that the scenarios incorporate the major funding and market liquidity risks to which the bank is exposed. These include risks associated with its business activities, products (including complex financial instruments and off-balance sheet items) and funding sources.

The defined scenarios should allow the bank to evaluate the potential adverse impact these factors can have on its liquidity position. While historical events may serve as a guide, a bank's judgment also plays an important role in the design of stress tests. Banks should conduct stress tests to assess the level of liquidity they should hold, the extent and frequency of which should be commensurate with the size of the bank and their specific business activities/liquidity for a period over which it is expected to survive a crisis. Banks are encouraged to have stress tests with various survival horizons in mind say one month or less; two or three months; and six months or more, etc.

Measuring and managing funding requirement can be done through two approaches.

- Stock approach.
- Flow approach.

7.9.1 Stock Approach: Stock approach is based on the level of assets and liabilities as well as off-balance sheet exposures on a particular date. The following ratios are calculated to assess the liquidity position of a bank. Banks may monitor these ratios by putting in place an internally defined limit approved by the board for these ratios. The industry averages for these ratios are given for information of banks. They may fix their own limits, based on their liquidity risk management capabilities, experience and profile. The stock ratios are meant for monitoring the liquidity risk at the solo bank level. Banks may also apply these ratios for monitoring liquidity risk in major currencies, viz. US Dollar, Pound Sterling, Euro and Japanese Yen at the solo bank level.

7.9.2 Flow Approach: Flow approach measurement involves comprehensive tracking of cash flow mismatches. For measuring and managing net funding requirements, the format prescribed by the RBI i.e. the statement of structural liquidity under ALM System for measuring cash flow mismatches at different time bands should be adopted. The cash flows are required to be placed in different time bands based on the residual maturity of the cash flows or the projected future behaviour of assets, liabilities and off-balance sheet items. The difference between cash inflows and outflows in each time period thus becomes a starting point for the measure of a bank's future liquidity surplus or deficit, at a series of points of time. Presently, banks are required to prepare domestic structural liquidity statement (Rupee) on a daily basis and report to RBI on a fortnightly basis. Further, structural liquidity statements in respect of overseas operations are also reported to RBI on a quarterly basis. Tolerance levels/prudential limits for various maturities may be fixed by the bank's top management depending on the bank's asset-liability profile, extent of stable deposit base, the nature of cash flows, regulatory prescriptions, etc. In respect of mismatches in cash flows in the near term, say up to 28 days, it should be the endeavour of the bank's management to keep the cash flow mismatches at the minimum levels.

Banks should analyse the behavioural maturity profile of various components of on-/off-balance sheet items on the basis of assumptions and trend analysis supported by time series analysis. The behavioural analysis, for example, may include the proportion of maturing assets and liabilities that the bank can rollover or renew, the behaviour of assets and liabilities with no clearly specified maturity dates, potential cash flows from off-balance sheet activities, including draw down under loan commitments, contingent liabilities and market related transactions. Banks should undertake variance analysis, at least once in six months to validate the assumptions used in the behavioural analysis. The assumptions should be fine-tuned over a period which facilitate near reality predictions about future behaviour of on-/off-balance sheet items.

Banks should also track the impact of prepayments of loans, premature closure of deposits and exercise of options built in certain instruments which offer put/call options after specified times. Thus, cash outflows can be ranked by the date on which liabilities fall due, the earliest date a liability holder could exercise an early repayment option or the earliest date.

As assumptions play critical role in projections of cash flows and measuring liquidity risk, assumptions used should be reasonable, appropriate and adequately documented. They should be transparent to the board/risk management committee and periodically reviewed.

7.10 Liquidity Management Framework in India

The liquidity management framework in India stands on two broad mutually reinforcing pillars of forward looking assessment. Pillar I is an assessment of the likely evolution of system-level liquidity demand based on near-term (four to six weeks) projections of autonomous drivers of liquidity. This forms the basis for taking decisions on use of discretionary liquidity absorbing/injecting measures to ensure that the liquidity conditions remain consistent with the goal of aligning money market rates to the policy repo rate. Pillar II is an assessment of system-level liquidity over a relatively longer time horizon, focusing on the likely growth in broad money, bank credit and deposits, the corresponding order of base money expansion and this assessment is then juxtaposed with a breakdown into autonomous and discretionary drivers of liquidity derived under Pillar I. Thus, Pillar II becomes the broader information set within which decisions relating to discretionary liquidity management measures are taken on the basis of Pillar I assessment.

7.10.1 Pillar I: The core of Pillar I is near-term forecasts of autonomous drivers of liquidity, particularly demand for currency (which reflects behaviour of households), demand for excess reserves (which reflects behaviour of the banking system), and the central government's balances with the RBI (which depends on cash flows of the Government). Large fluctuations in the central government's balances with the RBI leads to corresponding automatic expansion/contraction in the RBI's balance sheet, which has a magnifying impact on the overall monetary conditions.

For the purpose of liquidity management, forex market intervention is also an autonomous driver of liquidity, but since there cannot be any near term forecasts for these interventions, they are considered on information as available, i.e. backward looking, impacting liquidity evolution on t+2 settlement basis. The extent of volatility seen in the major frictional drivers of liquidity has been large, which poses the challenge of generating credible and precise short-term forecasts of liquidity demand in the system. Nevertheless, using a combination of forward looking information and a backward looking assessment of the time series evolution of the frictional determinants of liquidity, projections are generated on a regular basis to inform the RBI's decisions on discretionary liquidity management.

The RBI's discretionary liquidity management operations (primarily in the form of OMOs and changes in CRR, and also in terms of fixing limits for term repos and overnight repo amounts) is guided by the extent of LAF deficit that is 'reasonable' at any point of time, and the assessment of drivers of LAF deficit/surplus, i.e., whether frictional or structural.

7.10.2 Pillar II: Broad money growth that is consistent with inflation and growth projections at the beginning of the year and reviewed from time to time in a state-contingent manner provides leads about the growth in base money that will be required in the system during the course of the year. After accounting for autonomous drivers of liquidity and borrowed reserves (i.e., access to LAF by banks), assessment of the amount of discretionary liquidity management operations becomes possible, given the desirable evolution of the base money path as also the extent of LAF deficit/surplus relative to a norm (communicated in the form of +/- one per cent of NDTL).

Rigid adherence to base money rule is avoided due to uncertainties surrounding the relationship between monetary aggregates and the ultimate goal variables. Empirical estimates point to some improvement in the sensitivity of money demand to changes in the interest rate, thus providing the rationale for anchoring the operating framework with an interest rate rule. Currently, trajectories of monetary aggregates are only referred to as 'indicative'. The Reserve Bank revised its liquidity management framework with effect from September 5, 2014, with more frequent 14-day term repos and daily overnight variable rate repo operations, to ensure flexibility, transparency and predictability in liquidity management operations.

The Reserve Bank of India released Draft Guidelines on Liquidity Risk Management and Basel III Framework on Liquidity Standards for comments and feedback. The important points have been explained above. To address the deficiencies witnessed in liquidity risk management in the recent crisis and to strengthen liquidity risk management in banks, the Basel Committee on Banking Supervision (BCBS) published "Principles for Sound Liquidity Risk Management and Supervision" in September 2008. This was followed by the publication of "Basel III: International Framework for Liquidity Risk Measurement, Standards and Monitoring" in

December 2010 i.e., the Basel III rules text on liquidity prescribing two minimum global regulatory standards viz. liquidity coverage ratio (LCR) and net stable funding ratio (NSFR) for liquidity risk and a set of five monitoring tools.

The Reserve Bank, being a member of the BCBS, is fully committed to the objective of the Basel III reform package and, therefore, intends to implement these proposals for banks operating in India. Accordingly, draft guidelines on liquidity risk management and Basel III Framework on Liquidity Standards have been prepared.

The draft guidelines incorporate various instructions/guidance on liquidity risk management that the Reserve Bank of India has issued from time to time in the past, and where appropriate, harmonizes and enhances these instructions/guidance in line with the BCBS's Principles for Sound Liquidity Risk Management and Supervision. Additionally, Basel III guidelines on liquidity risk as will be applicable to the Indian banks have also been laid down. Two minimum global regulatory standards viz. LCR and NSFR as set out in the Basel III rules text issued by the BCBS in December 2010 have been prescribed under the guidelines which will become binding from 1 January 2015 and 1 January 2018, respectively. Till then, these guidelines have been issued for compliance on best effort basis. Banks are expected to submit the liquidity returns under the Basel III framework to the Reserve Bank from the month/quarter ending June 2012.

8

Managing Market Risks

8.1 Market Risk: Conceptual Settings

Market risk is one of the most important risks. Banks have long faced the risk of losses from undesirable market movements because they have several activities and undertake transactions that result in market exposure. Market risk exposure may be explicit in portfolios of securities/equities and instruments that are actively traded. Conversely, it may be implicit such as interest rate risk due to mismatch of loans and deposits. Besides, market risk may also arise from activities categorized as off-balance sheet item. Therefore, market risk is the potential for loss resulting from adverse movement in market risk factors such as interest rates, forex rates, equity and commodity prices. Market risk is the risk that the financial instrument's value will fluctuate as a result from market price changes, regardless of whether these changes are caused by factors typical for individual instruments or their issuer (counterparty), or by factors pertaining to all the instruments traded on the market.

The four most common factors connected with market risk are interest rates, currency exchange rates, costs of investments in trade portfolio (regardless of the instruments' character—debt or capital), prices of exchange commodities and other market variables related to the bank's activity. The market risk pertaining to both individual financial instruments and portfolio instruments can be a function of one, several or all these factors, and in many cases it can be very complicated. In general, market risk can be defined as a risk arising from market movements—of prices, interest rates and currency exchange rates.

Market risk is defined as the risk of losses in the value of a bank's trading portfolio due to changes in market factors such as interest rates, stock prices, exchange rates, inflation, economic growth, unemployment etc. This is also referred to as price risk.

Bank for International Settlements defines market risk as "the risk of losses in on- and off-balance sheet positions arising from movements in market prices". The risks subject to this requirement are:

- The risks pertaining to interest rate-related instruments and equities in the trading book.
- Foreign exchange risk throughout the banking corporation.

In this respect, the main factors contributing to market risk are equity, interest rate, foreign exchange, and commodity risk. However, just knowing what constitutes market risk is of little value unless we are able to appropriately quantify it and maintain adequate capital provisions for it.

Market risk is the risk that the value of an investment will decrease due to moves in market factors. The total market risk is the aggregation of all risk factors (Sironi and Resti, 2007; Dowd, 2002). Market risk can impact a company's business in many different ways. Exposure to market risk may arise as a result of the bank taking deliberate speculative positions or may come from the bank's market-making, dealer activities. For example, operating margins can be eroded due to the rising prices of raw materials or depreciating currencies in countries in which a company has foreign sales (direct market risk impact). Changes in the market environment may eventually force companies to adjust the prices of their products or services, potentially altering sales volumes or competitiveness, depending on the positioning and market exposures of the company's competitors (the indirect impact of market risk on business results). Some organizations may be paid to take market risks (e.g., financial organizations), but most seek to manage the impact of market risk on financial results (Gallati, 2003).

Given the increasing involvement of banks in investment

and trading activities combined with the high volatility of the market environment, the timely and accurate measurement of market risk is a necessity (Dowd, 2002). Trading activities require highly skilled analytical support. Traders must use some form of technical analysis to gauge market movements and market opportunities.

A fundamental analysis of classes of securities and of market behaviour is also needed for the trader to be able to anticipate price movements and position the portfolio accordingly. Ex-post analysis is also important to understand how market movements have affected profit and loss.

There is also the possibility for an investor to experience losses due to factors that affect the overall performance of the financial markets. Market risk, also called 'systematic risk', cannot be eliminated through diversification, though it can be hedged against. The risk that a major natural disaster will cause a decline in the market as a whole is an example of market risk. Other sources of market risk include recessions, political turmoil, changes in interest rates and terrorist attacks.

Investopedia explains market risk as, "the two major categories of investment risk are market risk and specific risk. Specific risk, also called 'unsystematic risk', is tied directly to the performance of a particular security and can be protected against through investment diversification. One example of unsystematic risk is that a company, whose stock you own will declare bankruptcy, thus making your stock worthless".

8.2 Market Risk Management Framework

According to the Basel committee, market risk is the risk that the value of an investment will decrease due to moves in market factors. Market risk is often propagated by other forms of financial risk such as credit and market liquidity risks. A bank should develop a sound and well informed strategy to manage market risk. The strategy should first determine the level of market risk the institution is prepared to assume. This level should be set with consideration given to, among other factors, the amount of market risk capital set aside by the institution. Once its market risk tolerance is determined, the institution should develop a strategy that balances its business goals with its market risk appetite. A bank should consider the following factors:

1. Economic and market conditions and their impact on market risk.
2. Whether the institution has the expertise to profit in specific markets and is able to identify, monitor and control the market risk in those markets.
3. The institution's portfolio mix and how it would be affected if more market risk was assumed. The four standard market risk factors include:

- Equity risk, or the risk that stock prices will change.
- Interest rate risk, or the risk that interest rates will change.
- Currency risk, or the risk that foreign exchange rates will change.
- Commodity risk, or the risk that commodity prices (i.e. grains, metals, etc.) will change.

Sometimes, a fifth risk factor is also considered—equity index risk, or the risk that stock or other index prices will change adversely. Even volatility risk is sometimes included in this.

Market risk encompasses the risk of financial loss resulting from movements in market prices. Market risk is rated, based upon, but not limited to, an assessment of the following evaluation factors:

- The sensitivity of the financial institution's earnings or the economic value of its capital to adverse changes in interest rates, foreign exchanges rates, commodity prices, or equity prices.
- The ability of management to identify, measure, monitor, and control exposure to market risk given the institution's size, complexity, and risk profile.
- The nature and complexity of interest rate risk exposure arising from non-trading positions.

- Where appropriate, the nature and complexity of market risk exposure arising from trading and foreign operations.

Risk taking is an integral part of the banking business. It is important for banks to find a balance between the risk a bank is willing to take and the returns it is expecting to achieve, while at the same time maintaining the sound financial position of the bank. Risk management seeks to address this.

The risk management system established should be commensurate with the size and complexity of a bank's business operations to ensure that the bank's risks could be managed according to the bank's risk strategy and appetite.

Market risk management involves the following questions:

- What are the risks?
- What would be the effect of risks on the profit and loss?
- How can we monitor and control price risk?
- Can we reduce the risks?

Management processes for market risk management are designed essentially to answer these questions. Accordingly, management processes are sub-divided into the following parts: (i) risk identification; (ii) risk measurement; (iii) risk monitoring and control, and (iv) risk mitigation.

Hence, management of market risk needs an organisation structure in place that can carry out the functions required for this purpose because management of market risk is a major concern of top management of banks. Following are the elements of market risk management.

8.2.1 Board and Senior Management Oversight: Like other risks, the concern for management of market risk must start from the top management. Effective board and senior management oversight of the bank's overall market risk exposure is the cornerstone of risk management process. For this part, the board of directors have following responsibilities.

- Delineate bank's overall risk tolerance in relation to market risk.
- Ensure that bank's overall market risk exposure is maintained at prudent levels and consistent with the

available capital.

- Ensure that top management as well as individuals responsible for market risk management, possess sound expertise and knowledge to accomplish the risk management function.
- Ensure that the bank implements sound fundamental principles that facilitate the identification, measurement, monitoring and control of market risk.
- Ensure that adequate resources (technical as well as human) are devoted to market risk management.

The first element of risk strategy is to determine the level of market risk the institution is prepared to assume. The risk appetite in relation to market risk should be assessed keeping in view the capital of the institution as well as exposure to other risks. Once the market risk appetite is determined, the institution should develop a strategy for market risk-taking in order to maximize returns while keeping exposure to market risk at or below the pre-determined level. While articulating market risk strategy, the board needs to consider economic and market conditions, and the resulting effects on market risk; expertise available to profit in specific markets and their ability to identify, monitor and control the market risk in those markets; and the institution's portfolio mix and diversification.

Finally, the market risk strategy should be periodically reviewed and effectively communicated to the relevant staff. There should be a process to identify any shifts from the approved market risk strategy and target markets, and to evaluate the resulting impact. The board of directors (BoD) should periodically review the financial results of the institution and, based on these results, determine if changes need to be made to the strategy.

While the board gives the strategic direction and goals, it is the responsibility of the top management to transform those directions into procedural guidelines and policy document and ensure proper implementation of those policies. Accordingly, senior management is responsible to:

- Develop and implement procedures that translate business policy and strategic direction set by BoD into operating standards that are well understood by bank's personnel.
- Ensure adherence to the lines of authority and responsibility that board has established for measuring, managing, and reporting market risk.
- Oversee the implementation and maintenance of management information system that identify, measure, monitor, and control bank's market risk.
- Establish effective internal controls to monitor and control market risk.

The institutions should formulate market risk management policies which are approved by the board. The policy should clearly delineate the lines of authority and the responsibilities of the board of directors, senior management and other personnel responsible for managing market risk; set out the risk management structure and scope of activities; and identify risk management issues, such as market risk control limits, delegation of approving authority for market risk control limit setting and limit excesses.

8.2.2 Organizational Structure: The organizational structure used to manage market risk varies depending upon the nature, size and scope of business activities of the institution. However, any structure does not absolve the directors of their fiduciary responsibilities of ensuring safety and soundness of the institution. While the structure varies depending upon the size, scope and complexity of business, at a minimum, it should take into account the following aspects.

- The structure should conform to the overall strategy and risk policy set by the BoD.
- Those who take risk (front office) must know the organization's risk profile, products that they are allowed to trade, and the approved limits.
- The risk management function should be independent, reporting directly to senior management or the BoD.
- The structure should be reinforced by a strong MIS for

controlling, monitoring and reporting market risk, including transactions between an institution and its affiliates.

Besides the role of board, as discussed earlier, a typical organization set up for market risk management should include:

- Risk management committee.
- Asset-liability management committee (ALCO).
- Middle office.

8.2.3 Risk Management Committee: It is generally a board level sub-committee constituted to supervise overall risk management functions of the bank. The structure of the committee may vary in banks depending upon the size and volume of the business. Generally, it could include heads of credit, market and operational risk management committees. It will decide the policy and strategy for integrated risk management, containing various risk exposures of the bank including the market risk. The responsibilities of risk management committee with regard to market risk management aspects include:

1. Devising policies and guidelines for identification, measurement, monitoring and control of all major risk categories.
2. The committee also ensures that resources allocated for risk management are adequate, given the size, nature and volume of the business and the managers and staff that take, monitor and control risk, possess sufficient knowledge and expertise.
3. The bank has clear, comprehensive and well-documented policies and procedural guidelines relating to risk management and the relevant staff fully understands those policies.
4. Reviewing and approving market risk limits, including triggers or stop losses for traded and accrual portfolios.
5. Ensuring robustness of financial models and the effectiveness of all systems used to calculate market risk.

6. The bank has robust management information system relating to risk reporting.

8.2.4 Asset-Liability Committee: Popularly known as ALCO, it is a senior management level committee responsible for supervision/management of market risk (mainly interest rate and liquidity risks). The committee generally comprises of senior managers from treasury, chief financial officer, business heads generating and using the funds of the bank, credit, and individuals from the departments having direct link with interest rate and liquidity risks. The CEO or some senior person nominated by CEO should be the head of the committee. The size as well as composition of ALCO could depend on the size of each institution, business mix and organizational complexity. To be effective, ALCO should have members from each area of the bank that significantly influences liquidity risk. In addition, the head of the information system department (if any) may be an invitee for building up of MIS and related computerization. Major responsibilities of the committee include:

1. To keep an eye on the structure/composition of bank's assets and liabilities and decide about product pricing for deposits and advances.
2. Decide on required maturity profile and mix of incremental assets and liabilities.
3. Articulate interest rate view of the bank and deciding on the future business strategy.
4. Review and articulate funding policy.
5. Decide the transfer pricing policy of the bank.
6. Evaluate market risk involved in launching of new products.

ALCO should ensure that risk management is not confined to collection of data. Rather, it will ensure that detailed analysis of assets and liabilities is carried out so as to assess the overall balance sheet structure and risk profile of the bank. The ALCO should cover the entire balance sheet/business of the bank while carrying out the periodic analysis.

8.2.5 Middle Office: The risk management functions relating to treasury operations are mainly performed by middle office. The concept of middle office has recently been introduced so as to independently monitor, measure and analyse risks inherent in treasury operations of banks. Besides, the unit also prepares reports for the information of senior management as well as bank's ALCO. Basically, the middle office performs risk review function of day-to-day activities. Being a highly specialized function, it should be staffed by people who have relevant expertise and knowledge. The methodology of analysis and reporting may vary from bank to bank depending on their degree of sophistication and exposure to market risks. These same criteria will govern the reporting requirements demanded of the middle office, which may vary from simple gap analysis to computerized VaR modelling.

Middle office staff may prepare forecasts (simulations) showing the effects of various possible changes in market conditions related to risk exposures. Banks using VaR or modelling methodologies should ensure that its ALCO is aware of and understand the nature of the output, how it is derived, assumptions and variables used in generating the outcome and any shortcomings of the methodology employed. Segregation of duties should be evident in the middle office, which must report to ALCO independently of the treasury function. In respect of banks without a formal middle office, it should be ensured that risk control and analysis should rest with a department with clear reporting independence from treasury or risk taking units, until normal middle office framework is established.

8.3 Market Risk Measurement

Accurate and timely measurement of market risk is necessary for proper risk management and control. The market risk measures seek to capture variations in market value arising out of uncertainties associated with various risk elements. These provide an objective measure of market risk in a transaction or of a portfolio. Market risk factors that affect the value of traded portfolios and the income stream or value of non-traded portfolio and other business activities should be identified and quantified using data that can be directly observed in markets or implied from observation or history. While there is a wide range of risk measurement techniques ranging from static measurement techniques (Gap analysis) to highly sophisticated dynamic modelling (Monte Carlo Simulation), the banks may employ any technique depending upon the nature, size and complexity of the business and most important, the availability and integrity of data. Banks may adopt multiple risk measurement methodologies to capture market risk in various business activities; however management should have an integrated view of the overall market risk across products and business lines. The measurement system ideally should:

- Assess all material risk factors associated with a bank's assets, liabilities, and off-balance sheet positions.
- Utilize generally accepted financial concepts and risk measurement techniques.
- Have well documented assumptions and parameters. It is important that the assumptions underlying the system are clearly understood by risk managers and top management. Market risk measures are based on:
- Sensitivity.
- Downside potential.

Sensitivity is measured as change in market value due to unit change in the variable. For example, where market value of a portfolio changes by ₹ 1,00,000 for 1 percent change in the rate of interest, interest rate sensitivity of the portfolio is 1,00,000. This gives us a measure of risk associated with the portfolio vis-à-vis change in the rate of interest. This measure suffers from the fact that it does not consider impact of other parameters, which may also change simultaneously. Secondly, the measure does not remain constant for all the values of the variable.

In case of downside potential, risk materializes only when earnings deviate adversely. Downside potential only captures possible losses ignoring profit potential. Downside risk is the most comprehensive measure of risk as it integrates sensitivity and volatility with the adverse effect of uncertainty. This is a measure that is most relied upon by banking and financial service industry as also the regulators.

8.3.1 Risk Monitoring: Risk monitoring processes are established to evaluate the performance of bank's risk strategies/policies and procedures in achieving overall goals. Whether the monitoring function is performed by middle office or it is a part of bank's internal audit, it is important that the monitoring function should be independent of units taking risk and report directly to the top management/board. Banks should have an information system that is accurate, informative and timely to ensure dissemination of information to management to support compliance with board policy. Reporting of risk measures should be regular and should clearly compare current exposures to policy limits. Further, past forecast or risk estimates should be compared with actual results to identify any shortcomings in risk measurement techniques. The board on a regular basis should review these reports. While the types of reports for board and senior management could vary depending upon the overall market risk profile of the bank, at a minimum, the following reports should be prepared.

- Summaries of bank's aggregate market risk exposure.
- Reports demonstrating bank's compliance with policies and limits.
- Summaries of finding of risk reviews of market risk policies, procedures and the adequacy of risk measurement system including any findings of internal/external auditors or consultants.

8.3.2 Risk Control: Bank's internal control structure ensures the effectiveness of process relating to market risk management. Establishing and maintaining an effective system of controls including the enforcement of official lines of authority and appropriate segregation of duties, is one of the management's most important responsibilities. Persons responsible for risk monitoring and control procedures should be independent of the functions they review. Key elements of internal control process include internal audit and review and an effective risk limit structure.

Banks need to review and validate each step of market risk measurement process. This review function can be performed by a number of units in the organization including internal audit/control department or ALCO support staff.

8.3.3 Risk Limits: As stated earlier, it is the board that has to determine bank's overall risk appetite and exposure limit in relation to its market risk strategy. Based on these tolerances the senior management should establish appropriate risk limits. Risk limits for business units, should be compatible with the institution's strategies, risk management systems and risk tolerance. The limits should be approved and periodically reviewed by the board of directors and/or senior management, with changes in market conditions or resources, prompting a reassessment of limits. Institutions need to ensure consistency between the different types of limits.

8.3.4 Gap Limits: The gap limits expressed in terms of interest sensitive ratio for a given time band aims at managing potential exposure to a bank's earnings/capital due to changes in interest rates. Setting such limits is a useful way to limit the volume of a bank's repricing exposures and is an adequate and effective method of communicating the risk profile of the bank to senior management.

Such gap limits can be set on a net notional basis (net of asset/liability amounts for both on- and off-balance sheet items) or a duration-weighted basis, in each time band. (Duration is the weighted average term to maturity of a security's cash flow. For instance, a ₹ 100, 5 year, 8 percent (semi-annual) coupon bond having a yield of 8 percent will have a duration of 4.217 years.

8.3.5 Factor Sensitivity Limits: The factor sensitivity of interest rate position is calculated by discounting the position using current market interest rate and then using the current market interest rate increase or decrease by one basis point. The difference in the two values known as factor sensitivity is the potential for loss given one basis point change in interest rate. Banks may introduce such limits for each time band as well as total exposure across all time bands. The factor sensitivity limit or PV01 limit measures the change in portfolio's present value given one basis point fluctuation in the underlying interest rate.

8.4 Market Risk Management Information System

For banks to make effective business and risk management decisions, it is critical that they be able to aggregate timely and accurate data for reporting on a variety of risk types. As the financial and regulatory environment becomes increasingly complex, this capability within the banks is important to senior decision-makers. They need the proper information to make judgments about the strategic direction of their banks, to help set risk appetite and to manage risk according to rapidly changing economic or market conditions.

Banks should establish and maintain a market risk management information system with adequate technological support and processing capacity to effectively measure and report the market risk exposed to the bank. The market risk management system should be operated in a prudent and consistently effective manner.

An effective market risk management information system should have the capability to produce timely, accurate and reliable reports for the board, senior management, specialized committees, risk-taking units and risk management and control units. These reports should be used to support decision-making at different levels (e.g., strategy formulation and risk budgeting), and to enable early identification of emerging market risk.

Inadequate information systems may hinder the ability of banks to manage broad financial risks as market events unfold rapidly and intensely.

The level of sophistication of the market risk management system should depend on the nature, characteristics, scale and complexity of the bank's business activities that expose the bank to market risk.

Generally it should be capable of:

- Measuring the market risks of a product or transaction in accordance with the measurement methods or models approved to be adopted by the bank.
- Aggregating data on a product, trading venue, counterparty, portfolio, trading unit and sub-unit, currency, etc.
- Supporting customized identification and aggregation of risk concentrations within the bank.
- Incorporating hedging and other risk mitigating actions to be carried out while taking into account related risks embedded.
- Reporting excesses in limits and policy exceptions, and alerting management of risk exposures approaching pre-set limits.
- Producing information and reports at appropriate intervals, or on an ad-hoc basis in times of stress.
- Conducting sensitivity analysis, back testing of risk measurement, stress testing or other market risk analysis required to be performed by the market risk management function.

The market risk management information system may be developed internally by the bank.

8.5 Modern Approaches to Market Risk Measurement

The policy for market risk control and management should be subordinated to several main aims:

- To protect the bank against unexpected losses and to contribute to income stability via independent identification, assessment and understanding of business market risks;

- To contribute to bringing the bank's organizational structure and management process in line with the best international practices and to set minimum standards for market risks control;
- To create transparent, objective and consistent information system of the market risks as a base for reasonable decision-making;
- To establish a structure that will help the bank to realize the connection between the business strategy and the operations on one hand, and between the purposes of risk control and monitoring, on the other.

The admissible threshold of market risk is the amount of potential unexpected loss which the bank is willing to assume because of unexpected and unfavourable changes in the market variables. The admissible threshold of market risk should not exceed the losses which the bank can assume without disturbing its financial stability. The bank's ability to overcome losses caused by market risk depends on its capital and reserves, on the potential losses originating from other non-market risks and on the regulatory capital required for maintaining the business activity.

Risk monitoring is fundamental for effective management process. That is the reason why banking institutions should have adequate internal reporting systems, reflecting their exposure to market risk. Sufficiently detailed regular reports should be submitted to the top management and to the various management levels.

There are significant differences in the internal and external views of what is a satisfactory market risk measure. Internally, bank managers need a measure that allows active, efficient management of the bank's risk position. Bank regulators want to be sure that bank's potential for catastrophic net worth loss is accurately measured and that the bank's capital is sufficient to survive such a loss. Both managers and regulators want up-to-date measures of risk. For banks active in trading, this may mean selective intraday risk measurement as well as a daily measurement of the total risk of the bank. However, the intraday measures that are relevant for asset allocation and hedging decisions are measures of the marginal effect of a trade on total bank risk and not the stand-alone riskiness of the trade. Regulators, on the other hand, are concerned with the overall riskiness of a bank and have less concern with the risk of individual portfolio components.

The need for a total risk measure implies that risk measurement cannot be decentralized. For parametric measure of risk, such as standard deviation, this follows from the theory of portfolio selection and the well-known fact that the risk of a portfolio is not, in general, the sum of that component risks. More generally, imperfect correlation among portfolio component implies that simulations of portfolio risk must be driven by the portfolio return distribution, which will not be invariant to changes in portfolio composition. Finally, given the costly regulatory capital requirements, choices among alternative assets require managers to consider risk/return or risk/cost trade-offs, where risk is measured as the change in portfolio risk resulting from a given change in portfolio composition. The appropriate risk scaling measure depends on the type of change being made.

Risk measurement is costly and time consuming. Consequently, bank managers compromise between measurement precision on the one hand and the cost and timeliness of reporting on the other. This trade-off will have a profound effect on the risk measurement method a bank will adopt.

Market risk can be measured by using two very sophisticated and quantitative methods known as value at risk (VAR) and stress testing (also known as scenario analysis).

8.5.1 Value at Risk (VaR) Method: The concept of VaR was first introduced in the regulatory domain in 1996 (BIS, 1996) in the context of measuring market risk. However, post-

1996 literature has given ample demonstration that the same concept is also applicable to much wider class of risk categories, including credit and operational risks. Today, VaR is considered as a unified risk measure and a new benchmark for risk management. Interestingly, not only the regulators and banks but many private sector groups also have widely endorsed statistical-based risk management systems, such as VaR.

Market risk is typically measured using a value at risk methodology. Value at risk is well established as a risk management technique, but it contains a number of limiting assumptions that constrain its accuracy. The first assumption is that the composition of the portfolio measured remains unchanged over the single period of the model. For short time horizons, this limiting assumption is often regarded as acceptable. For longer time horizons, many of the transactions in the portfolio may mature during the modelling period. Intervening cash flow, embedded options, changes in floating interest rates, and so on are ignored in this single period modelling technique.

Market risk can also be contrasted with specific risk, which measures the risk of a decrease in one's investment due to a change in a specific industry or sector, as opposed to a market-wide move.

The basic concept was nicely described by Linsmeier and Pearson (1996), "value at risk is a single, summary, statistical measure of possible portfolio losses. Specifically, value at risk is a measure of losses due to 'normal' market movements. Losses greater than the value at risk are suffered only with a specified small probability. Subject to the simplifying assumptions used in its calculation, value at risk aggregates all of the risks in a portfolio into a single number suitable for use in the boardroom, reporting to regulators, or disclosure in an annual report. Once one crosses the hurdle of using a statistical measure, the concept of value at risk is straight forward to understand. It is simply a way to describe the magnitude of the likely losses on the portfolio.

VaR is one of the most popular models in the industry, used both by institutions for internal risk management, and by regulators to dictate regulatory capital requirements. Value at risk (VaR) is one of the most popular methods of market risk analysis, but it is by no means a remedy for all ills.

Value at risk (VaR) analysis uses asset return distributions and predicted return parameters to estimate potential portfolio losses. In value at risk, it is the loss that portfolio will experience under distress. The loss is taken over time horizon: a day, a month, sometimes even one year. Distress is quantified by a percentile of the P&L function, usually 95 percent or 99 percent.

8.5.2 Stress Testing: Stress testing is a valuable risk management tool which tries to quantify the size of potential losses under certain stress events. A stress event is an exceptional but credible event to which a bank's portfolio is exposed. A stress event may involve subjecting the risk factors to shocks which itself is extreme but plausible movement of risk factor. In other words, it is a computer simulation technique that measures market risk over a certain period of time under abnormal market conditions. Stress tests provide information, summarizing the firm's exposure to extreme, but possible circumstances (Hughes and Macdonald, 2002).

It identifies and manages situations which can cause extraordinary losses by revaluing the portfolio under simulated conditions. In other words, in scenario analysis, the analyst postulates, changes the underlying determinants of portfolio value (e.g., interest rates, exchange rates, equity prices, and commodity prices) and revalues the portfolio, given those changes. The resulting change in value is the loss estimate. A typical procedure, often called stress testing, is to use a scenario based on a historically adverse and market move. This approach has the advantage of not requiring a distributional assumption for the risk calculation. On the other hand, it is subjective and incorporates a strong assumption that future financial upsets will strongly resemble those of the past. Stress testing covers many techniques such as:

1. Simple sensitivity test.
2. Scenario analysis.
3. Maximum loss.
4. Extreme value theory.

A. Simple Sensitivity Test: It isolates the short-term impact on a portfolio's value of a series of pre-defined moves in a particular market risk factor.

B. Scenario Analysis: It specifies the shocks that might affect a number of market risk factors simultaneously if an extreme, but possible, event occurs. It seeks to assess the potential consequences for a firm of an extreme, but possible, state of the world. Scenario analysis can be based on historical or a hypothetical event. This analysis is currently the leading stress testing technique.

C. Maximum Loss Approach: It assesses the risks of a portfolio by identifying the most potentially damaging combination of moves of market risk factors.

D. Extreme Value Theory: It is a means to better capture the risk of loss in extreme but possible circumstances. It is a statistical theory based on the behaviour of the 'tails' (i.e. the very high and low potential values) of probability distributions.

Bank's stress tests should be both of a quantitative and qualitative nature, incorporating both market risk and liquidity risk aspects of market disturbances. Quantitative criteria should identify plausible stress scenarios to which banks could be exposed. Qualitative criteria should emphasise that two major goals of stress testing are to evaluate the capacity of the bank's capital to absorb potential large losses and to identify steps the bank can take to reduce its risk and conserve capital. This assessment is integral to setting and evaluating the bank's strategy and the results of stress testing should be routinely communicated to senior management and, periodically, to the bank's board of directors.

A good stress test should:

- Be relevant to the current position.
- Consider changes in all relevant market rates.
- Examine potential regime shifts (whether the current risk parameters will hold or breakdown).
- Consider market illiquidity.
- Consider the interplay of market and credit risk.

9

Foreign Exchange Risks

Exchange rate risks arise because of international business being done in an environment where no uniform or universally acceptable currency is there. India is now well-integrated with the world economy and moves in tandem with global developments, both on the economic front as well on the currency front. The far-reaching changes in the Indian economy since liberalization in the early 1990s have had a deep impact on the Indian financial sector. The developments in the Indian foreign exchange (FX) derivatives market should be seen along with the steps taken to gradually reform the Indian financial markets. The resultant spurts in foreign investments led to substantial increase in the quantum of inflows and outflows in different currencies, with varying maturities. The reforms provided the economic rationale for the introduction of foreign exchange (FX) derivatives and risk management since then has under gone a paradigm shift.

9.1 Foreign Exchange Market

With globalisation, many changes have taken place in the economy. Raising of capital from the international markets has assumed significant proportion during the recent years. The volume of finance raised from international capital market is steadily increasing over the last few years, across the national boundaries. New institutions are emerging on the international financial scenario and new derivative financial instruments (products) to cater to the requirements of multinational organisations and the foreign investors have been introduced. The Government of India has opened up the Indian economy to foreign investments and has taken a number of bold and drastic measures to globalise the Indian economy. Various fiscal, trade and industrial policy decisions have been taken and new avenues provided to foreign investors including foreign institutional investors (FIIs) and NRIs etc., for investment, especially in infrastructural sectors like power and telecommunication.

For this, we must understand the meaning of foreign exchange market, risks associated with these and the types of accounts in inter-bank transactions.

The foreign exchange market is a market in which individuals, firms and banks buy and sell foreign currencies or foreign exchange. The purpose of the foreign exchange market is to permit transfers of purchasing power denominated in one currency to another i.e. to trade one currency for another.

Transfer of purchasing power is necessary because international trade and capital transactions usually involve parties living in countries with different national currencies.

Each party wants to trade and deal in his own currency but since the trade can be invoiced only in a single currency, the parties mutually agree on a currency beforehand. The currency agreed could also be any convenient third country currency such as the US dollar. For example, if an Indian exporter sells machinery to a UK importer, the exporter could invoice in pound, rupees or any other convenient currency like the US dollar.

9.2 Nostro, Vostro and Loro Accounts

In inter-bank transactions, foreign exchange is transferred from one account to another account and from one centre to another centre. Therefore, the banks maintain three types of current accounts in order to facilitate quick transfer of funds in different currencies. These accounts are nostro, vostro and loro accounts meaning "our", "your" and "their". A bank's foreign currency account maintained by the bank in a foreign country and in the home currency of that country is known as nostro account or "our account with you". For example, an Indian bank's Swiss franc account with a bank in Switzerland. Vostro account is the local currency account maintained by a foreign bank/branch. It is also called "your account with us". For example, an Indian rupee account maintained by a bank in Switzerland with a bank in India. The loro account is an account wherein a bank remits funds in foreign currency to another bank for credit to an account of a third bank.

9.3 Types of Foreign Exchange Risks

There are different views of various authors on the subject. Some of the authors are of the view that an organisation's exposure to exchange rate risk is not relevant, so organisations therefore should not manage their exposure. They support their argument by quoting purchasing power parity agreement theory, meaning that any change in exchange rate should be matched by price movements. Another argument they quote for exchange rate irrelevance is that investors in MNCs could hedge the risk on their own. Exchange rates cannot be forecasted perfectly, but the corporate managers at least can measure the exposure to exchange rate fluctuations. This risk can be classified into three types.

9.3.1 Transaction Risk: It is observed when movements in the price of a currency upwards or downwards results in a loss on a particular transaction. This exposure is also known as conversion exposure. The degree to which the value of future cash transactions can be affected by exchange rate fluctuations is known as transaction exposure. A firm has *transaction exposure* whenever it has contractual cash flows (receivables and payables) whose values are subject to unanticipated changes in exchange rates due to a contract being denominated in a foreign currency.

To realize the domestic value of its foreign-denominated cash flows, the firm must exchange foreign currency for domestic currency. As firms negotiate contracts with set prices and delivery dates in the face of a volatile foreign exchange market with exchange rates constantly fluctuating, the firms face a risk of changes in the exchange rate between the foreign and domestic currency. It refers to the risk associated with the change in the exchange rate between the time an enterprise initiates a transaction and settles it.

Applying public accounting rules causes firms with transactional exposures to be impacted by a process known as 're-measurement'. The current value of contractual cash flows is re-measured at each balance sheet date. If the value of the currency of payment or receivable changes in relation to the firm's base or reporting currency from one balance sheet date to the next, the expected value of these cash flows will change. U.S. accounting rules for this process are specified in ASC 830, originally known as FAS 52. Under ASC 830, changes in the value of these contractual cash flows due to currency valuation changes will impact the current income. There are two steps involved in measuring transaction exposure. These are: (i) determine the projected net amount of cash flow; and (ii) determine the overall risk of exposure to that currency. Corporate managers of MNCs may select one of the hedging technique so as to eliminate transaction exposure. These are: (a) forward hedge; (b) future hedge; (c) money market hedge; and (d) currency option hedge.

9.3.2 Translation Risk: It is also known as accounting exposure. It arises due to adverse exchange rate movements and change in the level of investments and borrowings in foreign currency. A firm's *translation exposure* is the extent to which its financial reporting is affected by exchange rate movements. As all firms generally must prepare consolidated financial statements for reporting purposes, the consolidation process for multinationals entails translating foreign assets and liabilities or the financial statements of foreign subsidiary/ subsidiaries from foreign to domestic currency. While translation exposure may not affect a firm's cash flows, it could have a significant impact on a firm's reported earnings and therefore its stock price. Translation exposure is distinguished from transaction risk as a result of income and losses from various types of risk having different accounting treatments.

The following exposures are also taken into account:

A. Economic Exposure: A firm has *economic exposure* (also known as *forecast risk*) to the degree that its market value is influenced by unexpected exchange rate fluctuations. Such exchange rate adjustments can severely affect the firm's market share position with regard to its competitors, the firm's future cash flows, and ultimately the firm's value. Economic exposure can affect the present value of future cash flows. Any transaction that exposes the firm to foreign exchange risk also exposes the firm economically, but economic exposure can be caused by other business activities and investments which may not be mere international transactions, such as future cash flows from fixed assets. A shift in exchange rates that influences the demand for a good in some country would also be an economic exposure for a firm that sells that good.

B. Contingent Exposure: A firm has *contingent exposure* while bidding for foreign projects or negotiating other contracts or foreign direct investments. Such an exposure arises from the potential for a firm to suddenly face a transactional or economic foreign exchange risk, contingent on the outcome of some contract or negotiation. For example, a firm could be waiting for a project bid to be accepted by a foreign business or government that if accepted would result in an immediate receivable. While waiting, the firm faces a contingent exposure from the uncertainty as to whether or not that receivable will happen. If the bid is accepted and a receivable is paid the firm then faces a transaction exposure, so a firm may prefer to manage contingent exposures.

Currency risk is the possibility that exchange rate changes will alter the expected amount of principal and return of the lending or investment. At times, banks may try to cope with this specific risk on the lending side by shifting the risk associated with exchange rate fluctuations to the borrowers. However, the risk does not get extinguished, but only gets converted into credit risk. By setting appropriate limits, open position and gaps, stop-loss limits, day light as well as overnight limits for each currency, individual gap limits and aggregate gap limits, clear cut and well defined division of responsibilities between front, middle and back office, the risk element in foreign exchange can be managed/monitored.

9.3.3 Country Risk: International trade is prone to country risk, due to chances of loss in cross-border trades, which can be caused by events in a particular country, affecting the probability of the business or recovery of trade credits or investments. This is the risk that arises due to cross-border transactions that are growing dramatically in the recent years owing to economic liberalization and globalization. It is the possibility that a country will be unable to service or repay debts to foreign lenders on time. In country risk, the buyers are unable to meet the commitment due to restrictions imposed on transfer of funds by the foreign government or regulators.

When the transactions are with the foreign government the risk is called as sovereign risk. It comprises of transfer risk arising on account of possibility of losses due to restrictions on external remittances; sovereign risk associated with lending to government of a sovereign nation or taking government guarantees; political risk when political environment or legislative process of country leads to government taking over the assets of the financial entity (like nationalization, etc.) and preventing discharge of liabilities in a manner that had been agreed to earlier; cross-border risk arising on account of the borrower being a resident of a country other than the country where the cross-border asset is booked; and currency risk, a possibility that exchange rate change, will alter the expected amount of principal and return on the lending or investment. In the process, there can be a situation in which seller (exporter) may deliver the goods, but may not be paid or the buyer (importer) might have paid the money in advance but was not delivered the goods for one or the other reasons.

As per the RBI guidance note on country risk management, banks should reckon both fund and non-fund exposures from their domestic as well as foreign branches, if any, while identifying, measuring, monitoring and controlling country risk. It advocates that banks should also take into account indirect country risk exposure. For example, exposures to a domestic commercial borrower with large economic dependence on a certain country may be considered as subject to indirect country risk. The exposures should be computed on a net basis, i.e. gross exposure minus collaterals, guarantees etc.

Netting may be considered for collaterals in/guarantees issued by countries in a lower risk category and may be permitted for bank's dues payable to the respective countries. RBI further suggests that banks should eventually put in place appropriate systems to move over to internal assessment of country risk within a prescribed period by which time the new capital accord would be implemented.

The system should be able to identify the full dimensions of country risk as well as incorporate features that acknowledge the links between credit and market risks. Banks should not rely solely on rating agencies or other external sources as their only country risk-monitoring tool. With regard to inter-bank exposures, the guidelines suggests that banks should use the country ratings of international rating agencies and broadly classify the country risk rating into six categories such as insignificant, low, moderate, high, very high and off-credit. However, banks may be allowed to adopt a more conservative categorization of the countries. Banks may set country exposure limits in relation to the bank's regulatory capital (Tier I and II) with suitable sub-limits, if necessary, for products, branches, maturity etc. Banks were also advised to set country exposure limits and monitor such exposure on weekly basis before eventually switching over to real tie monitoring. Banks should use variety of internal and external sources as a means to measure country risk and should not rely solely on rating agencies or other external sources as their only tool for monitoring the country risk. Banks are expected to disclose the "country risk management" policies in their annual reports by way of notes.

9.3.4 Currency Risk: An organisation which operates in a foreign market has a currency exposure. The risk to such organisation is that its cash flows are likely to be affected by fluctuations in exchange rate. "Foreign currency risk' has been defined by ED of IFAC as, 'foreign currency exposure and risk management' is the net potential gain or loss which can arise from exchange rate changes to the foreign currency exposures of an organisation'. The relaxation of exchange controls and the liberalization of cross-border capital movements have fuelled a tremendous growth in international financial markets. The volume and growth of global foreign exchange trading has far exceeded the growth of international and capital flows and has contributed to greater exchange rate volatility and therefore the currency risk.

Currency risk results from changes in exchange rates and originates in mismatches between the values of assets and liabilities denominated in different currencies (Grath, 2008). This mismatch may cause a bank to experience losses as a result of adverse exchange rate movements when the bank has an open on- or off-balance sheet position, either spot or forward, in an individual foreign currency. In recent years, a market environment with freely floating exchange rates has practically become the global norm. This has opened the doors for speculative trading opportunities and has increased currency risk. For example, in the case of a net long position in foreign currency, domestic currency depreciation will result in a net gain for a bank and appreciation will produce a loss. Under a net short position, exchange rate movements will have the opposite effect.

The fluctuations in the value of domestic currency creating currency risk are normally motivated by macroeconomic factors manifest over long periods of time. Among the factors affecting these fluctuations are the volume and directions of a country's trade and capital flows. But the fluctuations are also influenced by expected or unexpected political events, changed expectations on the part of market participants, or speculation based currency trading may also give rise to currency changes. All these factors affect the supply and demand for the currency and therefore the movement of the exchange rate in the currency market (Grath, 2008).

A bank has a net position in foreign currency and is exposed to currency risk when its assets and liabilities are not equal in a given currency. Banks should have written policies to govern their activities in foreign currencies and to limit their exposure to currency risk and therefore to potential incurred losses.

In principle, limits are established based on the nature of currency risk and the type of business by which that risk is incurred.

Risk in a banking context arises from any transaction or business decision that contains uncertainty concerning the result. Because virtually every bank's transaction is associated with some level of uncertainty, nearly every transaction contributes to the overall risk of a bank.

All of the risks enumerated and many more lead to possible fluctuations in the bank's income statement or profitability and hence the value of the bank. As a general rule, event risk has a much larger impact on a company's cash flows and value than continuous risk (Schroeck, 2002).

Currency risk, a possibility that exchange rate change, will alter the expected amount of principal and return on the lending or investment. Floating exchange rate arrangement has brought in its wake pronounced volatility, adding a new dimension to the risk profile of banks' balance sheets. The increased capital flows across free economies following deregulation have contributed to increase in the volume of transactions. Large cross-border flows together with the volatility has rendered the banks' balance sheets vulnerable to exchange rate movements. Dealing in different currencies brings opportunities as also risks. If the liabilities in one currency exceed the level of assets in the same currency, then the currency mismatch can add value or erode value depending upon the currency movements. The simplest way to avoid currency risk is to ensure that mismatches, if any, are reduced to zero or near zero. Banks undertake operations in foreign exchange like accepting deposits, making loans and advances and quoting prices for foreign exchange transactions. Irrespective of the strategies adopted, it may not be possible to eliminate currency mismatches altogether. Besides, some of the institutions may take proprietary trading positions as a conscious business strategy.

Managing currency risk is one more dimension of asset-liability management. Mismatched currency position besides exposing the balance sheet to movements in exchange rate also exposes it to country risk and settlement risk. Ever since the RBI (Exchange Control Department) introduced the concept of end of the day near square position in 1978, banks have been setting up overnight limits and selectively undertaking active day time trading. Following the introduction of 'Guidelines for Internal Control over Foreign Exchange Business' in 1981, maturity mismatches (gaps) are also subject to control. Following the recommendations of Expert Group on Foreign Exchange Markets in India (Sodhani Committee), the calculation of exchange position has been redefined and banks have been given the discretion to set up overnight limits linked to maintenance of additional Tier-I capital to the extent of 5 percent of open position limit.

9.3.5 Foreign Exchange Settlement Risk: When dealing with foreign exchange transactions, the issue of settlement risk often arises. Foreign exchange settlement risk is the risk of loss when a bank in a foreign exchange transaction pays the currency it sold but does not receive the currency it bought. Settlement risk exists for any traded product, but the size of the foreign exchange market makes foreign exchange transactions the greatest source of settlement risk for many market participants. In light of the aforementioned, a bank should have systems that provide appropriate and realistic estimates of foreign exchange exposures on a timely basis. These systems would include policies and procedures similar to those mentioned previously with emphasis on understanding settlement risk and formulating a clear and firm plan on its management.

A bank's procedures for managing its foreign exchange settlement risks should be commensurate with the range and scope of its activities. However, in all cases and regardless of the settlement method used, foreign exchange settlement risk management should begin at the highest levels of the organisation, with a policy on foreign exchange settlement risk from the bank's board of directors. This policy should be an integral and consistent part of the bank's overall policy towards counter party risk. It should be regularly reviewed and, where necessary, modified to take account of new circumstances such as changes in the scale or nature of the bank's foreign exchange operations or in the method of settlement used.

Senior management should exercise appropriate oversight of settlement exposures. Although specific organisational approaches may vary across banks, foreign exchange settlement risk management should be integrated into the overall risk management process. Managing foreign exchange settlement risk involves many different functional areas of a bank, including trading, credit, operations, legal, risk assessment, branch management, and correspondent relations. In larger, more complex banks, counter party exposures may also run across departments, branches and legal entities, and may encompass multiple product lines, such as lending and foreign exchange trading. Banks should have clear procedures for measuring and managing exposures that provide for the efficient aggregation of all components of credit risk toward a counter party. This is a prerequisite for the proper functioning of the overall risk management process.

Specific foreign exchange risk practices may differ among banks depending upon factors such as the institution's size, and the nature and complexity of its activities. However, a comprehensive foreign exchange risk programme should deal with, at a minimum, good management information systems, contingency planning and other managerial and analytical techniques. In this area, there is considerable difference in current practice. This can be explained by the different franchises that coexist in the banking industry. Most banking institutions view activity in the foreign exchange market beyond their franchise, while others are active participants. The former will take virtually no principal risk, no forward open positions, and have no expectations of trading volume. Within the latter group, there is a clear distinction between those that restrict themselves to acting as agents for corporate and/or retail clients and those that have active trading positions.

The most active banks in this area have large trading accounts and multiple trading locations. And, for these, reporting is rather straight forward. Currencies are kept in real time, with spot and forward positions marked-to-market. As is well known, however, reporting positions is easier than measuring and limiting risk. Here, the latter is more common than the former. Limits are set by desk and by individual trader, with monitoring occurring in real time by some banks, and daily closing at other institutions.

As a general characterization, those banks with more active trading positions tend to have invested in the real-time VaR systems, but there are exceptions. Limits are the key elements of the risk management systems in foreign exchange trading as they are for all trading businesses. As discussed, it is fairly standard for limits to be set by currency for both the spot and forward positions in the set of trading currencies. At many institutions, the derivation of exposure limits has tended to be an imprecise and inexact science. For these institutions, risk limits are set currency-by-currency by subjective variance tolerance.

Others, however, do attempt to derive the limits using a method that is analytically similar to the approach used in the area of interest rate risk. Even for banks without a VaR system in place, stress tests are done to evaluate the potential loss associated with changes in the exchange rate. This is done for small deviations in exchange rates but it also may be investigated for historical maximum movements. The latter is investigated in two ways. Either historical events are captured, and worse-case scenario simulated, or the historical events are used to estimate a distribution from which the disturbances are drawn. In the latter case, a one or two standard deviation change in the exchange rate is considered.

While some use these methods to estimate volatility, until recently, most did not use variability in setting individual currency limits, or in the aggregating exposure across multiple correlated currencies. Incentive systems for foreign exchange traders are another area of significant differences between the average commercial bank and its investment banking counterpart. While, in the investment banking community trader performance is directly linked to compensation, this is less true in the banking industry.

While some admit to significant correlation between trader income and trading profits, many argue that there is absolutely none. This latter group tends to see such linkages leading to excess risk taking by traders who gain from successes but do not suffer from losses. Accordingly, to their way of thinking, risk is reduced by separating foreign exchange profitability and trader compensation.

9.4 Foreign Exchange Risk Management Framework

Once a firm recognizes its exposure, it then has to deploy resources in managing it. A heuristic for firms to manage this risk effectively and which can be modified to suit firm-specific needs i.e. some or all, the following tools could be used.

9.4.1 Forecasts: After determining its exposure, the first step for a firm is to develop a forecast on the market trends and what the main direction/trend is going to be on the foreign exchange rates. The period for forecasts is typically 6 months.

It is important to base the forecasts on valid assumptions. Along with identifying trends, a probability should be estimated for the forecast coming true as well as how much the change would be.

9.4.2 Risk Estimation: Based on the forecast, a measure of the value at risk (the actual profit or loss for a move in rates according to the forecast) and the probability of this risk should be ascertained. The risk that a transaction would fail due to market-specific problems should be taken into account. Finally, the systems risk that can arise due to inadequacies such as reporting gaps and implementation gaps in the firms' exposure management system should be estimated.

9.4.3 Benchmarking: Given the exposures and the risk estimates, the firm has to set its limits for handling foreign exchange exposure. The firm also has to decide whether to manage its exposures on a cost centre or profit centre basis. A cost centre approach is a defensive one and the main aim is to ensure that cash flows of a firm are not adversely affected beyond a point. A profit centre approach on the other hand is a more aggressive approach where the firm decides to generate a net profit on its exposure over time.

9.4.4 Hedging: Based on the limits a firm sets for itself to manage exposure, the firm then decides an appropriate hedging strategy. There are various financial instruments available for the firm to choose from: futures, forwards, options and swaps and issue of foreign debt. Hedging strategies and instruments are explored in a separate section.

9.4.5 Stop Loss: The firm's risk management decisions are based on forecasts which are but estimates of reasonably unpredictable trends. It is imperative to have stop loss arrangements in order to rescue the firm if the forecasts turn out wrong. For this, there should be certain monitoring systems in place to detect critical levels in the foreign exchange rates for appropriate measures to be taken.

9.4.6 Reporting and Review: Risk management policies are typically subjected to review, based on periodic reporting. The reports mainly include profit/loss status on open contracts after marking to market, the actual exchange/interest rate achieved on each exposure, and profitability vis-à-vis the benchmark and the expected changes in overall exposure due to forecasted exchange/ interest rate movements. The review analyses whether the benchmarks set are valid and effective in controlling the exposures, what the market trends are and finally whether the overall strategy is working or needs change.

9.5 Methods of Foreign Exchange Risk Management

Exposure management techniques are classified into internal and external techniques according to their basic origin. Internal techniques are mainly used as a part of company's regulatory financial management and aims at minimizing its exposure to exchange risk. These basically aim at reducing or preventing an exposed position from arising.

The external techniques are used to provide protection against the possibility that exchange losses will result from the foreign exchange risk exposure which the internal measures have not been able to eliminate. These consist of basically the contractual measures to provide protection against an exchange loss which may arise from an existing translation or exposed position. There are internal action and external action techniques for risk management.

9.5.1 Internal Techniques

A. Netting: Netting implies offsetting exposures in one currency with exposure in the same or another currency, where exchange rates are expected to move high in such a way that losses or gains on the first exposed position should be offset by gains or losses on the second currency exposure. It is of two types: bilateral netting and multilateral netting. In bilateral netting, each pair of subsidiaries nets out their own positions with each other. Flows are reduced by the lower of each company's purchases from or sales to its netting partner.

B. Leading and Lagging: It refers to the adjustment of inter-company credit terms—leading means a prepayment of a trade obligation and lagging means a delayed payment. It is basically inter-company technique whereas netting and matching are purely defensive measures. Inter-company leading and lagging is a part of risk-minimizing strategy or an aggressive strategy that maximizes expected exchange gains. Leading and lagging requires a lot of discipline on the part of participating subsidiaries. Multinational companies which make extensive use of leading and lagging may either evaluate subsidiary performance in a pre-interest basis or include interest charges and credits to overcome evaluation problem.

Another important complicating factor in leading and lagging is the existence of local minority interests. If there are powerful local shareholders in the 'losing' subsidiary, there will be strong objections because of the added interest cost and lower profitability which results from the consequent local borrowing. Government by implementing credit and exchange controls, may restrict such operations.

C. Matching: The netting is typically used only for inter-company flows arising out of groups' receipts and payments. As such, it is applicable only to the operations of a multinational company rather than exporters or importers. In contrast, matching applies to both third parties as well inter-company cash flows. It can be used by the exporter/importer as well as the multinational company. It refers to the process in which a company matches its currency inflows with its currency outflows with respect to amount and timing. Receipts generated in a particular currency are used to make payments in that currency and hence, it reduces the need to hedge foreign exchange risk exposure. Hedging is required for unmatched portion of foreign currency cash flows. The aggressive company may decide to take forward cover on its currency payables and leave the currency receivables exposed to exchange risk; if forward rate looks cheaper than the expected spot rate.

In matching operation, the basic requirement is a two-way cash flow in the same foreign currency. This kind of operation is referred to as natural matching. Parallel matching is another possibility. In parallel matching, gains in one foreign currency are expected to be offset by losses in another, if the movements in two currencies are parallel. In parallel matching, there is always the risk that if the exchange rates move in opposite direction to expectations, both sides of the parallel match leads to exchange losses or gains.

D. Pricing Variation: In order to manage foreign exchange risk exposure, there are two types of pricing tactics: price variation and currency of invoicing policy. One way for companies to protect themselves against exchange risk is to increase selling price to offset the adverse effects of exchange rate fluctuations. Selling price requires the analysis of competitive situation, customer credibility, price controls and internal delays.

E. Trading or Financing Pattern: Inter-company or transfer price variation refers to the arbitrary pricing of inter-company transfer of goods and services at a higher or lower rate than the market price. In establishing international transfer prices, one tries to satisfy a number of objectives. The firms want to minimize taxes and at the same time win approval from the government of the host country.

Yet, the basic objectives of profit maximization and performance evaluation are also significant. Often, it is not possible to satisfy all these objectives simultaneously, so a company must decide which objectives are more important. As a result, particular transfer price may be established arbitrarily to fulfil the objective involving international considerations. For the strong currency exporter, the defensive approach is the only option available for export invoicing since the home currency is probably the strongest currency acceptable to the customer.

For the weak currency exporter, however, there may be significant gains from an aggressive currency-of-invoicing policy. In such circumstances, foreign currency invoicing may be attractive to the exporter in expectation that the home currency equivalent sale proceeds would be changed by a foreign currency appreciation over the credit period. However, there are risks involved in switching from a weak currency to a stronger one. The relative strengths of the two currencies could reverse themselves in the future and hence currency of invoicing cannot be changed regularly. Price list adjustment and loss of customer's credibility are hindrances in changing currency of billing.

F. Asset and Liability Management: This technique can be used to manage balance sheet, income statement and cash flow exposures. It can also be used aggressively or defensively. The aggressive approach reflects to increase in exposed assets, revenues, and cash inflows denominated in strong currencies and to increase in exposed liabilities, expenses, and cash outflows in weak currencies. The defensive firm will seek to minimize foreign exchange gains and losses by matching the currency denomination of assets/liabilities, revenues/expenses and cash inflows/outflows, irrespective of the distinction between strong and weak currencies. To archive these objectives, variables are grouped. Operating variables includes trade receivables and payables, inventory and fixed assets and financial variables, cash, short-term investments and debt.

The currency denomination of operating variables is determined by intrinsic business conditions, production and marketing factors.

Financial variables can be used for exposure management purpose and thus corporate financial management has more discretion over currency denomination. The scarcity of currency finance is often a major problem. The parent company would borrow the weak currency for long-term while the subsidiary is usually restricted to short-term borrowing. This is because: (a) most subsidiaries are not individually listed on a stock exchange, so that the public issue of debt instruments is very difficult, hence, the bulk of long-term loans taken out by foreign subsidiaries are private placements; (b) many foreign subsidiaries are relatively small and not well known to the local financial community; and (c) host governments may be reluctant to allow term borrowing by expatriate subsidiaries.

9.5.2 External Techniques: External techniques are used by both exporters and importers as well as by multinational companies. The costs of the external exposure management methods are fixed and predetermined. The main external exposure management techniques are forward exchange contracts, short-term borrowing, discounting, forfeiting and government exchange risk guarantees.

A. Forward Exchange Contracts: Forward exchange contracts refer to agreements in which two parties agree upon the exchange rate at which currencies will be exchanged on future date or within future specified duration. Forward contracts reduces exchange risk element in the foreign transactions. Price is paid for the protectionism and best-cost alternative should be chosen to reduce the cost of purchase. There is, however, some disagreement on how to calculate cost of forward cover mainly because there are two kinds of costs involved, an ex-ante cost and an opportunity cost.

B. Forward Contracts: Forward cover can be used to hedge purchases as well as sales. It may be of two types, namely forward purchases cover and forward sales cover. Forward purchase cover is extended to have terms and conditions related to export of goods and services. Period of delivery of currency should not be beyond seven days of the probable date of receipt as per the purchase forward cover. It can be extended for purchases of proceeds of foreign currency notes from licensed full-fledged money changers, provided that the currency notes were exported through the bank, for realisation and credit to the bank's account. All other requirements related to export can be hedged by it. Forward sales cover imports of goods and services in India, where the import is permissible as per the Import Control Regulation and repayment of foreign currency loans approval from RBI for availing such loan must have been obtained.

Such approval should contain the details of currency, amount of interest and the repayment procedure. The forward contract would have to provide for repayment in accordance with settled terms and conditions. Repayment liabilities under such loans would be carried forward for several years and it would not be possible to fix the forward rate for such future dates as the market would not predict rate beyond six to seven months.

C. Options: Options are rights and not obligations to make buy and sell decision. An option is a contract between two parties known as the buyer and the seller or writer. The buyer pays a price or premium to the seller for the right but not the obligation to buy or sell a certain amount of a specified quantity of one currency in exchange at a fixed price for a specified period of time. The right to buy is a call option and the right to sell is a put option.

D. Futures: Futures are contracts to buy or sell financial instruments, for forward delivery or settlement on standardized terms and conditions. Future contacts are similar to forward contracts but are more liquid as these are traded on recognized exchanges.

E. Swaps: Swaps refer to a contract between two parties, termed as counter parties, who exchange payments between them for an agreed period of time according to certain specified rules. It is defined as a financial transaction involving two counter parties who agreed terms to exchange streams of payments or cash flows overtime on the basis of agreement at the beginning of the contract. Swap is like a series of forward contracts. Swaps involve a series of exchanges at specific future dates between the counter parties.

9.6 Foreign Exchange Market in India

In India, the foreign exchange market is a three-level structure consisting of: (a) Reserve Bank of India (RBI) at the top, (b) authorised dealers (ADs) licensed by the RBI, and (c) customers (exporters, importers, companies, and other foreign exchange earners). In addition to these main market players, there are foreign exchange money changers who bring buyers and sellers together, but are not permitted to deal in foreign exchange on their own account.

Dealings in the foreign exchange market include transactions between authorised dealers and the exporters/importers and other customers, transactions among authorised dealers themselves, transactions with overseas banks and transactions between authorised dealers and the RBI.

The mode of exchange rate determination is of paramount importance to the development of foreign exchange market. There is no single exchange rate regime which can be considered appropriate for all countries, at all times. Though the choice of an exchange rate regime is country-specific and contingent on macroeconomic policies, there is a growing consensus globally in favour of a flexible/floating rate regime.

9.6.1 Market Segments: The Indian foreign exchange market is a decentralised multiple dealership market comprising two segments—the spot and the derivatives market. In the spot market, currencies are traded at the prevailing rates and the settlement or value date is two business days ahead. The two-day period gives adequate time for the parties to send instructions to debit and credit the appropriate bank accounts at home and abroad.

The derivatives market encompasses forwards, swaps and options. Though forward contracts exist for maturities up to 1 year, majority of forward contracts are for 1 month, 3 months, or 6 months. Forward contracts for longer periods are not common because of the uncertainties involved and related pricing issues.

A swap transaction in the foreign exchange market is a combination of a spot and a forward in the opposite direction. The spot market is the dominant segment of the Indian foreign exchange market. The derivative segment of the foreign exchange market is assuming significance and the activity in this segment is gradually rising.

9.6.2 Market Players: Players in the Indian foreign exchange market include: (a) authorised dealers (ADs), mostly banks who are authorised to deal in foreign exchange, (b) foreign exchange brokers who act as intermediaries, and (c) customers—individuals and corporates who need foreign exchange for their transactions. Though customers are major players in the foreign exchange market, for all practical purposes they depend upon ADs and brokers. In the spot foreign exchange market, foreign exchange transactions were earlier dominated by brokers. However, the situation has changed with the evolving market conditions and as of now the transactions are dominated by ADs. Brokers continue to dominate the derivatives market.

The RBI intervenes in the market essentially to ensure orderly market conditions. The RBI undertakes sales/purchases of foreign currency in periods of excess demand/supply in the market.

Foreign Exchange Dealers' Association of India (FEDAI) plays a special role in the foreign exchange market for ensuring smooth and speedy growth of the foreign exchange market in all its aspects. All ADs are required to become members of the FEDAI and execute an undertaking to the effect that they would abide by the terms and conditions stipulated by the FEDAI for transacting in foreign exchange business. The FEDAI is also the accrediting authority for the foreign exchange brokers in the inter-bank foreign exchange market.

The licences for ADs are issued to banks and other institutions, on their request, under Section 10(1) of the Foreign Exchange Management Act, 1999. ADs are divided into different categories.

All scheduled commercial banks—which include public sector banks, private sector banks and foreign banks operating in India—belong to category I of the ADs.

All upgraded full-fledged money changers (FFMCs) and select regional rural banks (RRBs) and co-operative banks belong to category II of the ADs.

Select financial institutions such as EXIM Bank belong to category III of the ADs.

All merchant transactions in the foreign exchange market have to be necessarily undertaken directly through ADs. However, to provide depth and liquidity to the inter-bank segment, ADs have been permitted to utilise the services of brokers for better price discovery in their inter-bank transactions.

The customer segment of the foreign exchange market comprises major public sector units, corporates and business entities with foreign exchange exposure. It is generally dominated by select large public sector units such as Indian Oil Corporation (IOC), Oil and Natural Gas Commission (ONGC), Bharat Heavy Electrical Limited (BHEL), Steel Authority of India Limited (SAIL), Maruti Udyog and also the Government of India (for defence and civil debt service) as also big private sector corporates like Reliance Group, Tata Group and Larsen and Toubro, among others.

In recent years, foreign institutional investors (FIIs) have emerged as major players in the foreign exchange market.

9.6.3 Sources of Supply and Demand of Foreign Exchange: The major sources of supply of foreign exchange in the Indian foreign exchange market are receipts on account of exports and invisibles in the current account and inflows in the capital account such as foreign direct investment (FDI), portfolio investment, external commercial borrowings (ECBs) and non-resident deposits. In India, the Government has no foreign currency account, and thus the external aid received by the Government comes directly to the reserves and the RBI releases the required rupee funds. Hence, this particular source of supply of foreign exchange is not routed through the market and as such does not impact the exchange rate.

Demand for foreign exchange emanates from imports and

invisible payments in the current account, amortisation of ECBs (including short-term trade credits) and external aid, redemption of NRI deposits and outflows on account of direct and portfolio investment.

9.6.4 Derivative Market Instruments: Derivatives play a crucial role in developing the foreign exchange market as they enable market players to hedge against underlying exposures and shape the overall risk profile of participants in the market. Banks in India have been increasingly using derivatives for managing risks and have also been offering these products to corporates. In India, various informal forms of derivatives contracts have existed for a long time though the formal introduction of a variety of instruments in the foreign exchange derivatives market started only in the post-reform period, especially from mid-1990s. The foreign exchange derivative products that are now available in Indian financial markets can be grouped into three broad segments, viz. forwards, options (foreign currency rupee options and cross currency options) and currency swaps (foreign currency rupee swaps and cross currency swaps).

The most widely used derivative instruments are the forwards and foreign exchange swaps (rupee-dollar).

10

Risks in Insurance Business

10.1 Meaning of Risk in Insurance Business

Life is full of risks—some are preventable or can at least be minimized, some are avoidable and some are completely unforeseeable. What's important to know about risk when thinking about insurance is the type of risk, the effect of that risk, the cost of the risk and what one can do to mitigate the risk? Risk is an uncertain event or condition that if occurs, has a positive or negative effect on meeting the project objectives related to components such as schedule (time), cost, scope or quality.

Risk is unavoidable and present in every human situation. It is present in our daily lives and in public and private sector organizations. Depending on the context (insurance, stakeholder, technical causes), there are many accepted definitions of risk in use.

The common concept in all definitions is uncertainty of outcomes. Where they differ is in how they characterize the outcomes. Some describe risk as having only adverse consequences, while others are neutral.

One description of risk is the following: risk refers to the uncertainty that surrounds future events and outcomes. It is the expression of the likelihood and impact of an event with the potential to influence the achievement of an organization's objectives.

The phrase "the expression of the likelihood and impact of an event" implies that, as a minimum, some form of quantitative or qualitative analysis is required for making decisions concerning major risks or threats to the achievement of an organization's objectives. For each risk, two calculations are required: its likelihood or probability; and the extent of the impact or consequences.

Risk, as defined in insurance, is the probability of a loss. Risk sometimes denotes an object that is a cause of risk, or a person or property that would be risky to insure. Thus, a heavy drinker would be a risk as a driver, or a wooden building would be a poor risk for fire insurance. The profitability of any insurance company depends on how well it can predict losses; thus, assessing risk requires the accurate calculation of the probability of losses.

In insurance practice, risk is used for perils or loss producing events. Any risk bearing object needs to be insured so as to cover its unexpected losses caused by uncertain events. The degree of risk refers to the likelihood of occurrence of an event. It is a measure of accuracy with which the outcome of a chance event can be predicted.

Risk is a condition in which there exists a quantifiable dispersion in the possible outcomes from any activity. It can be classified in a number of ways.

According to Life Insurance Corporation of India, risk may be defined as, "a condition where there is a possibility of an adverse deviation from a desired outcome that is expected or hoped for—there is no requirement that the possibility be unmeasurable only that it must exist".

In most of the risky situations, the following elements are commonly found:

1. The outcome is uncertain i.e. there is a possibility that one or other(s) may occur. Therefore, there are at least two possible outcomes for a given situation.
2. Out of the possible outcomes, one is unfavourable or not liked by the individual or the analyst.

10.2 Risk and Uncertainty

Risk exists as a consequence of uncertainty and is present in all activities whatever the size or complexity and whatever industry or business sector. It is important to understand that risk is a broader concept. There is no single definition of risk. Economic risk (which we will refer to simply as risk) is the possibility of losing economic security. Most economic risks derive from variation from the expected outcome. Risk traditionally has been defined in terms of uncertainty. Risk has several meanings. In general, risk refers to the possibility or chance of meeting danger, suffering loss or injury or exposure to adversity or danger. In a broader sense, risk is uncertainty. Risk is defined as the possibility of loss or injury, and insurance is concerned with the degree of probability of loss or injury.

The concept of risk in insurance refers only to uncertainty on economic matters. Non-economic risks of respect, insult, prestige or love are not being dealt here. When risk is defined as uncertainty, some authors make a careful distinction between objective risk and subjective risk. Objective risk is (also called degree of risk) is defined as the relative variation of actual loss from expected loss. Objective loss declines as the number of exposures increases. Hence, objective risk varies inversely with square root of the number of cases under observation. Subjective risk is defined as uncertainty based on a person's mental condition or state of mind. The impact of subjective risk varies depending on the individual.

Uncertainty is often confused with the risk. Uncertainty refers to unknown result of an event. The result may be harmful or helpful to human interest. Uncertainty refers to a situation where the outcome is not certain or unknown. It refers to the state of mind characterised by doubt, based on the lack of knowledge about what will or what will not happen in future. Employees in insurance industry often use the term risk to identify the property or life being insured. Insurance provides protection from exposure to hazards and probability of loss. Uncertainty being a perceptual phenomenon, it implies different degrees to different persons. Risk can be defined as uncertainty regarding loss. To elaborate further:

- Inability to work and earn an income due to disability is a risk.
- Destruction of a home due to hurricane is a risk.

- Loss of family income due to death is a risk.
- Potential for an automobile accident is a risk.
- Chance of someone slipping on an icy driveway is a risk.

10.3 Loss Defined

A risk refers to a situation where there is a possibility of a loss. Loss has been defined in many ways. Loss refers to the act or instance of losing the detriment or a disadvantage resulting from losing. Loss means being without something previously possessed. Generally, the term *loss* is used to denote the absence of something previously possessed, such as lost time or lost opportunities as well as economic losses, such as a lost wallet. However, insurance uses only the more restricted definition of economic loss, since only economic losses are insurable risks. Hence, in insurance, a loss is the unexpected reduction in the economic value of one's possessions. Insurance companies use this definition because they can only cover such a loss with the payment of money. A loss differs from an expense, which is an expected payment for a good or service. Thus, buying fuel for the car is an expense, while a car accident is a loss.

Chance of loss refers to a fraction or the relative frequency of loss. It is the probability that a loss will occur, which can either be an expected loss or an actual loss, divided by the number exposed to loss, or the sample population. Because the chance of loss is only an average, actual losses may differ significantly from expected losses, especially for small samples, but as the sample size increases, actual and expected losses will tend to converge.

$$\text{Chance of Loss} = \frac{\text{Expected or Actual Loss}}{\text{Number of Possible Losses}}$$

Because the chance of loss is only an average, actual losses may differ significantly from expected losses, especially for small samples, but as the sample size increases, actual and expected losses will tend to converge.

10.4 Perils and Hazards

Risk is the chance of loss, and peril is the direct cause of the loss. If a house burns down, then fire is the peril. A peril refers to the cause of loss or the contingency that may cause a loss. Perils may be general or specific. A hazard is anything that either causes or increases the likelihood of a loss. Hazards are the conditions that increase the severity of loss or the conditions affecting perils. Hazards can be classified as follows: (i) physical hazards; and (ii) intangible hazards. A physical hazard is a physical condition that increases the possibility of a loss. Thus, smoking is a physical hazard that increases the likelihood of a house fire and illness. Intangible hazards are more or less psychological in nature like attitudes and culture. These can be further classified as follows.

Moral hazards are losses that result from dishonesty such as fraud. Thus, insurance companies suffer losses because of fraudulent or inflated claims. The American legal system is a moral hazard in that it motivates many people to sue simply for financial profits because of the enormous amount of money that can sometimes be won, and because there is little cost to the plaintiff, even if he loses. A good example is the asbestos litigation, which has bankrupted many companies, even though very few plaintiffs show any real evidence of disease, and are unlikely to ever develop any disease that can be shown, by the preponderance of the evidence, to have resulted from asbestos exposure. This type of moral hazard is often referred to as legal hazard. Legal hazard can also result from laws or regulations that force insurance companies to cover risks that they would otherwise not cover, such as including coverage for alcoholism in health insurance.

Insurance can be regarded as a morale hazard because it increases the possibility of a loss that results from the insured worrying less about losses. In other words, it refers to the attitude of indifference to take care of the property on the premise that a loss will be indemnified by the insurance company. Therefore, they take fewer precautions and may engage in risky activities—because they have insurance. Societal Hazards: Legal and Cultural—these refer to the increase in the frequency and severity of loss arising from societal customs and structure.

10.5 Elements of an Insurable Risk

Though insurance may be one of the most effective ways to handle risks, not all risks are insurable. As noted earlier, insurers will insure only pure risks, or those that involve only the chance of loss with no chance of game. For pure risk to be insurable, it should possess the following characteristics.

10.5.1 Loss Must be Definite and Measurable: The loss must be definite and measurable in money terms. An insurable risk must involve a loss that is definite as to the cause, time, place and amount. An insurer must be able to determine how much its liability will be, when it becomes payable. Loss of peace of mind, tension etc. or loss of life cannot be indemnified.

10.5.2 Loss Must be Statistically Predictable: The loss must be statistically predictable. This enables insurers to estimate the average frequency and severity of future losses and to set appropriate premium rates. (e.g. in life and health insurance). If there is no determinable distribution of premium, there is no question of issuing a cover by an insurance company.

10.5.3 Large Number of Exposure Units: The loss exposure to be insured must be large. There must be a sufficiently large pool to be insured and those in the pool must be grouped into classes with similar risks so the insurer is able to predict losses. Because the theory of insurance is based on law of large numbers, therefore the main necessity for a risk to be insurable is that there must be a sufficiently large number of homogeneous exposure in order that losses are reasonably predictable.

10.5.4 Loss Due to Chance: The loss must be due to chance. In order to be insurable, a risk must involve the chance of loss that is outside the insured's control. The insurer must be able to calculate both the average frequency and the average severity of future losses with some degree of accuracy.

10.5.5 Loss Cannot be Catastrophic: The losses should not be non-catastrophic. Insurers typically will not insure risks that will expose them to catastrophic losses. Insurers need to be reasonably certain that the losses will not exceed certain limits. Not all the units in homogeneous group will be subject to an adverse event.

10.5.6 Premium Should be Economically Feasible: The price charged by the insurer for buying the risk (i.e. premium) is generally much less than the face value or the amount of the policy called sum insured, though the insurance pool is structured to be sufficiently large. Thus, the insured must be able to afford to pay the premium.

Risk refers to the uncertainty that surrounds future events and outcomes. It is the expression of the likelihood and impact of an event with the potential to influence the achievement of an organization's objectives. Risk can be classified into following categories.

10.6 Pure and Speculative Risk

In insurance, risk refers only to uncertainty on economic matters. Non-economic risks of respect, insult, prestige or love are not being dealt here. There are two types of risk: (i) pure or static risks, and (ii) dynamic or speculative risks.

10.6.1 Pure or Static Risks: Pure risk is defined as a situation in which there are only the possibilities of loss or no loss. The only possible outcomes are adverse (loss) and neutral (no loss). Pure risk is the threat of loss with no chance for profit, such as the threat of fire, accident, or theft. If such events occur, a company loses money, but if they don't, the company gains nothing. Static risks involve those losses resulting from the destruction of an asset or changes in its possession as a result of dishonesty or human failure.

10.6.2 Speculative and Dynamic Risks: Speculative risk can result in either profit or loss. A firm takes on speculative risk by buying new machinery, acquiring more inventory or a new plant, and making other potentially profitable decisions in which the probability of loss may be relatively low and the amount of loss known. An entrepreneur's chance to make a profit is a speculative risk. Speculative risk can be defined as a situation in which either profit or loss is possible. Examples of these risks are:

- Management: (i) market (change of fashion, bad or good trading conditions); (ii) finance (loss of interest); and (iii) production (strike by workers).
- Political (war, bad foreign relations).
- Innovation (new business ventures' initial losses).

Hence,

Risk = Possibility of Loss.

Insurance = Probability of Loss.

Only pure risks are insurable because they involve only the chance of loss. They are pure in the sense that they do not mix both profits and losses. Both speculative risk and pure risk involve the possibility of loss. Speculative risk also involves the possibility of gain as well even if there is no loss. In conjunction with the two different types of risk, there are two concepts to become familiar with: (i) perils; and (ii) hazards. A peril is the cause of a risk. A peril is the immediate specific event causing loss and giving rise to risk. A hazard is the source of danger. The hazard is the underlying factor behind the peril that leads to the probability of a particular loss to the insurer. It is an active ingredient that could create a peril, which could then lead to a particular loss event.

It is important to distinguish between pure and speculative risks for three reasons. First, through the use of commercial, personal and liability insurance policies, insurance companies in the private sector generally insure only pure risks.

Speculative risks are not considered insurable, with some exceptions.

Second, the law of large numbers can be applied more easily to pure risks than to speculative risks. The law of large numbers is important in insurance because it enables insurers to predict loss figures in advance. It is generally more difficult to apply the law of large numbers to speculative risks in order to predict future losses. One of the exceptions is the speculative risk of gambling, where casinos can apply the law of large numbers in a very efficient manner.

Finally, society as a whole may benefit from a speculative risk even though a loss occurs, but it is harmed if a pure risk is present and a loss occurs. For instance, a computer manufacturer's competitor develops a new technology to produce faster computer processors more cheaply. As a result, it forces the other computer manufacturer into bankruptcy. Despite his bankruptcy, society as a whole benefits since the competitor's computers work faster and are sold at a lower price. On the other hand, society would not benefit when most pure risks, such as an earthquake, occurs.

10.7 Types of Pure Risks

There are various types of risks that affect individuals. These are as under:

- Personal risks.
- Property risks.
- Liability risks.

10.7.1 Personal Risks: These are risks that directly affect an individual. They involve the possibility of loss or reduction of income, of extra expenses, and the elimination of financial assets. There are four major personal risks:

- Premature death (dying too early).
- Old age.
- Poor health.
- Unemployment (loss of income may be temporary/ permanent, but routine living expenses continue).

10.7.2 Property Risks: These are the risks of having property damaged from numerous perils. Property loss can occur as a result of fire, lightening, windstorms, and a number of other causes. Property owners face the possibility of both direct and indirect (consequential) losses. If a car is damaged in a collision, the direct loss is the cost of repairs. If a firm experiences a fire in the warehouse, the direct cost is the cost of rebuilding and replacing inventory. Consequential or indirect losses are non-physical losses such as loss of business. Such losses include the time and effort required to arrange for repairs, the loss of use of the car or warehouse while repairs are being made, and the additional cost of replacement facilities or lost productivity. A property is exposed to losses because of accidents or catastrophes such as floods or hurricanes. Thus, a direct loss is defined as a financial loss that results from the physical damage, destruction etc. Whereas, an indirect loss is a financial loss that results indirectly from the occurrence of a direct physical damage or theft loss.

10.7.3 Liability Risks: These are another important type of pure risk that many people face. More than ever, we are living in a litigious society. One can be sued for any frivolous reason. One has to defend himself when sued, even when the suit is without merit. One is exposed to the possibility of liability loss (loss caused by a third party who is considered at fault) by having to defend against a lawsuit when he or she has in some way hurt other people. The responsible party may become legally obligated to pay for injury to persons or damage to property. Liability risk may occur because of catastrophic loss exposure or because of accidental loss exposure. These arise out of human mistakes.

10.8 Fundamental Risk and Particular Risk

Fundamental risks arise out of the nature of the society we live in or from some physical calamity beyond the control of man. A fundamental risk is one that is impersonal both in its origin and consequence. Fundamental risks affect the entire economy or large number of people or groups within the economy. Examples of fundamental risks are high inflation, unemployment, war, and natural disasters such as earthquakes, hurricanes, and floods. Hurricane Katrina was the largest single catastrophe in the history of United States. More recently, the risk of a terrorist attack is rapidly emerging as a fundamental risk.

A particular risk is a risk of a particular nature, has its origin in individual events. Particular risks are risks that affect only individuals and not the entire community. Examples of particular risks are burglary, theft, auto accident, dwelling fires. With particular risks, only individuals experience losses, and the rest of the community is left unaffected.

The distinction between a fundamental and a particular risk is important, since government assistance may be necessary in order to insure fundamental risk. Social insurance, government insurance programs, and government guarantees and subsidies are used to meet certain fundamental risks in our country. For example, the risk of unemployment is generally not insurable by private insurance companies but can be insured publicly by federal or state agencies. In addition, flood insurance is only available through and/or subsidized by the federal government.

10.9 Subjective and Objective Risks

Subjective risk refers to the mental state of an individual who experiences doubt or worry as to the outcome of a given event. As the term suggests, subjective risk can be defined as the degree of uncertainty perceived by an individual. It can therefore vary from one person to another. Subjective risk is essentially the psychological uncertainty that arises from an individual's mental attitude or state of mind.

Objective risk differs primarily in the sense that it is more precisely observable and therefore, measurable. Since objective risk can be statistically measured, it is a very powerful method for managing risk. As the number of exposure increases, the insurer is able to predict its future loss experience more precisely. This phenomenon is based on the law of large numbers. The law states that as the number of exposure increase, the variation reduces; therefore the actual loss experience will approach the expected loss experience.

10.10 Insurable and Uninsurable Risks

Insurable risks are those which after the selection process can be carried out by an insurer although there can be different terms and conditions for different policyholders. In other words, if the insurance company has enough statistics to work out the probability of the risk, it is called an insurable risk. An insurable risk follows the following guidelines:

- Policyholder must have an insurable interest.
- Loss must be measurable.
- Chance of loss must be measurable.
- Loss must be accidental.
- Insurance company's risk should be dispersed; that is, spread among different geographical areas so a flood or other natural disaster in one area will not bankrupt the insurance company.
- Insurance company must be able to set standards for accepting the risk.

Insurable risks are of three categories, such as:

- **Standard Risk**: This is related with the normal life where there is no much or no less risk. There is certain criteria on which the risks are judged as normal life.
- **Super-standard Risk**: This risk is present where there is lesser risk than the standard risk. It is also known as preferred risk.
- **Sub-standard Risk**: Sub-standard risks are those risks which are higher though insurable than the standard risk. The sub-standard risks are above the standard risk and below the uninsurable risk.

A risk is uninsurable when an insurance company cannot calculate the probability of the risk and therefore cannot work out a premium that the business must pay. If the insurance can be purchased at higher premium, there should not be any uninsurable risk. There are a number of reasons why some persons are not insurable. In order to protect existing policy-holders, the insurance company must accept those risks against which it can assess adequate and fair premiums to provide for claims.

This risk is too widespread and the loss is incurred due to our own deliberate actions, hence it cannot be insured. Consequential losses are also generally uninsurable.

10.11 Diversifiable Risk and Non-diversifiable Risk

Diversifiable risk is the risk which can be mitigated by investing in different companies, different sectors, different assets and also different regions. Here one can try to minimize the risk of huge loss by taking the whole risk against one or few companies/sectors/assets/regions.

Non-diversifiable risk cannot be mitigated at all. This is the risk which is exposed to in an individual investment. Every investment holds market risk, i.e. uncertainty of market moving up or down and respective movement of our investment. There is no specific method that can be used to handle the non-diversifiable risk. This is due to their impact which is reflected on the entire market.

10.12 Burden of Risk

The presence of risk results in certain social and economic effects which are undesirable because some losses will actually occur. When a wage earner dies or money is stolen or car is destroyed due to fire, there is a financial loss. These losses are the primary burden of risk. There are three major burdens/effects which are as follows:

- The size of an emergency fund should be increased.
- Effects on economic growth and capital accumulation.
- Feelings of worry, frustration and mental unrest.

There are some detrimental aspects of risk as well. The

uncertainty as to whether the loss will occur requires the prudent individual to prepare for its possible occurrence. In the absence of insurance, one way this can be done is to accumulate a reserve fund to meet the losses if they do occur. Accumulation of such a reserve fund carries an opportunity cost, for funds must be available at the time of the loss and must therefore be held in a liquid state. The return on such funds will presumably be less, than if they were put to alternate uses.

The existence of risk may have a detrimental effect on the economic growth and capital accumulation. Because the progress in an economy is determined to a large extent by the rate of capital accumulation but the investment of capital involves risk, that is distasteful. Many corporations have discontinued manufacturing certain products. Thus, consumers must pay the high cost for the goods and services.

Finally, a burden of risk is that worry, mental unrest and frustration are present. There are many examples that can illustrate these risks. Some passengers in a commercial vehicle may become nervous and fearful if the vehicle encounters severe turbulence during travelling. But in speculative risk, many individuals enjoy uncertainty connected with wagering more than the certainty of not gambling—otherwise he or she would not gamble. But there is a possibility of gain or profit, which exists only in speculative risk category.

10.13 Role of Risk Manager

The term risk manager in insurance can be used in a sense that a person who performs the risk management job, whether he is an employee of an organisation or an outsider as a consultant or an agent or a broker. It basically means an individual employed by an organisation who is responsible for the risk management function. The first step in effective risk management for any organization is to identify exposures to the potential accidental losses facing that particular organization—risk identification is one of the most crucial direct responsibilities of every risk manager. Therefore, most people primarily responsible for risk management in for-profit organizations spend a good deal of their work time with the basic tools of identifying loss exposures: accident reports and loss histories, financial statements, news reports of losses that have befallen other firms in their industry, flowcharts of the firm's operations, memos about actual and proposed changes within the firm, and—perhaps most importantly—personal inspections of the firm's facilities and operations. Risk managers are responsible for managing the risks to the organisation, its employees, customers, reputation, assets and interests of stakeholders. Various functions have been performed by the risk managers.

Risk manager has to be a specialised person to forecast and plan risk management.

Risk manager should have knowledge and skills to deal with the risks that an organisation may face.

Risk manager has to cooperate and communicate with various sections or departmental heads of the organisation to find the different risks and coordinate with the persons handling the risks.

Risk managers advise organisations on any potential risks to the profitability or existence of the company. They identify and assess threats, put plans in place for if things go wrong and decide how to avoid, reduce or transfer risks.

The risk manager has to:

- Provide a methodology to identify and analyse the financial impact of loss to the organization, employees, the public, and the environment.
- Prepare risk management and insurance budgets and allocate claim costs and premiums to departments and divisions.
- Provide for the establishment and maintenance of records including insurance policies, claim and loss experience.
- Assist in the review of major contracts, proposed facilities, and/or new program activities for loss and insurance implications.

However, it is the risk manager who ultimately decides how best to deal with these possible loss exposures from the suggestions offered. What is true for effective exposure identification in for-profit firms is even truer for non-profit firms.

The other key activities may include the following:

- Planning, designing and implementing an overall risk management process for the organisation;
- Risk assessment, which involves analysing risks as well as identifying, describing and estimating the risks affecting the business;
- Risk evaluation, which involves comparing estimated risks with criteria established by the organisation such as costs, legal requirements and environmental factors, and evaluating the organisation's previous handling of risks;
- Establishing and quantifying the organisation's 'risk appetite', i.e. the level of risk they are prepared to accept;
- Risk reporting in an appropriate way for different audiences, for example, to the board of directors so they understand the most significant risks, to business heads to ensure they are aware of risks relevant to their parts of the business and to individuals to understand their accountability for individual risks;
- Corporate governance involving external risk reporting to stakeholders;
- Carrying out processes such as purchasing insurance, implementing health and safety measures and making business continuity plans to limit risks and prepare for if things go wrong;
- Conducting audits of policy and compliance to standards, including liaison with internal and external auditors; and
- Providing support, education and training to staff to build risk awareness within the organisation.

In small organisations, the risk management job is confined to the president or the owner. In medium organisations, the risk handling job is entrusted to the chief financial officer or someone at middle level management position. In large organisations, the risk management department is headed by the top official, generally director, who is also a member of the board of directors and who is supported by an analyst, generally a professional who is entrusted with all risk research responsibilities. Below the chain are middle level managers designated by the respective risk management methods, viz., prevention and loss control, insurance etc.

The risk manager cannot be successful without the assistance of other groups within the organization. Full cooperation from departments' and divisions' staff is essential. Other managers must provide information necessary for the risk manager to review and identify loss exposures. Supervisors must be aware of their role in the prevention of loss and be accountable to follow procedures, attend risk control meetings, and, when appropriate, provide any recommended training. The scope of risk manager's job differs across organisations. In the broadest sense, the risk manager has the overall responsibility for all risk control and risk financing activities, including the organisation's employee benefit plan.

Bibliography

Bibliography

Alexander, C. (ed.) (2003), "Operational Risk: Regulation, Analysis and Management", Prentice Hall.

Bank for International Settlements (2003), "Sound Practices for the Management and Supervision of Operational Risk", Risk Management Group of the Basel Committee on Banking Supervision, February.

Bank for International Settlements (2009), "Revisions to the Basel II Market Risk Framework", Basel Committee on Banking Supervision.

Banerjee, S. and Banipal, K. (2005), "Managing Operational Risk: Framework for Financial Institutions", Working Paper, A.B Freeman School of Business, Tulane University, November.

Bessis, J. (2002), "Risk Management in Banking", John Wiley & Sons Ltd.

Dima, A.M. (2009), "Operational Risk Assessment Tools for Quality Management in Banking Services", *Amfiteatru Economic,* XI (26), pp. 364-372.

Dowd, Kevin (2002), "An Introduction to Market Risk Measurement", John Wiley & Sons Ltd.

Emmett Vaughan and Therese Vaughan (2002), "Essentials of Risk Management and Insurance", John Wiley & Sons Inc., New Jersey.

Fabozzi, F.J. and Konishi, A (1995), "Asset-Liability Management", S. Chand & Co., New Delhi.

Fabozzi, F.J., Mann, S.V. and Choudhry, M. (2003), "Measuring and Controlling Interest Rate and Credit Risk", 2nd edition, John Wiley & Sons Inc., New Jersey.

Gestel, Tony Van and Baesens, Bart (2009), "Credit Risk Management: Financial Risk Components, Rating Analysis, Models, Economic and Regulatory Capital", Oxford University Press Inc., New York.

Gupta, P. K. (2005), "Insurance and Risk Management", Himalaya Publishing House, Mumbai.

Harmantzis, F. (2002), "Operational Risk Management in Financial Services and the New Basel Accord", Working Paper, Stevens Institute of Technology, New Jersey.

Harrington and Niehaus (1999), "Insurance and Risk Management", McGraw Hill Inc., New York.

Harrington, R. (1987), "Asset and Liability Management by Banks", OECD, Paris.

Indian Institute of Banking and Finance (2010), "Banking and Financial Management", Mumbai.

Jackson, P. (1999), "Capital Requirements and Bank Behaviour: The Impact of the Basel Accord", Basel Committee on Banking Supervision Working Papers, Bank for International Settlements, Basel.

Kanchu, Thirupathi and Kumar, Manoj (2013), "Risk Management in Banking Sector: An Empirical Study", *International Journal of Marketing, Financial Services and Management Research*, Volume 2, No. 2, February.

Khanna, P.K. (2012), "Management of Banks", Himalaya Publishing House, Mumbai.

Kumar, Manoj and Yadav, Ghanshyam Chand (2013), "Liquidity Risk Management in Bank: A Conceptual Framework", *AIMA Journal of Management and Research,* Volume 7, Issue 2/4, May.

Kwan, S. and Eisenbeis, R.A. (1997), "Bank Risk, Capitalization, and Operating Efficiency", *Journal of Financial Services Research,* Kluwer Academic Publishers.

Mishra, R.N. (2004), "Basel II: Pillar 2-The Supervisory Review Process", *Professional Banker.*

Moosa, I.A. (2007), "Operational Risk Management", Palgrave Macmillan, Hampshire.

Murali, S. and Subbukrishna, K.R. (2008), "New Capital Framework in Indian Bank Credit Management", Himalaya Publishing House, Mumbai.

Narasimham Committee Reports on Banking, 1991.

Raghwan, R.S. (2003), "Risk Management in Banks", *Chartered Accountant*, February.

Rejda, G.E. (2002), "Principles of Risk Management and Insurance", Pearson Education Inc.

Scott, E. Harrington and Niehaus, Gregory R. (1999), "Insurance and Risk Management", Irwin/McGraw Hill.

Santomero, A.M. (1997), "Commercial Bank Risk Management: An Analysis of the Process", *Journal of Financial Services Research*, 12:2/3, pp. 83-115.

Sinkey, J.F. (1992), “Commercial Bank Financial Management”, 4th edition, Maxwell Macmillan, New York.

Trieschmann, J.C., Gistavson, S.G. and Hoyt, R.E. (2001), “Risk Management and Insurance”, South Western College Publishing.

Websites

www.rbi.org.in
www.bis.org
www.banksofindia.com
www.iupindia.org
www.economictimes.com
www.thehindubuisnessline.com
www.insurancetech.com
www.financial express.com
www.bimabazar.com
www.iosrjournals.org

Index

Index